CONTENTS

Notes on
English Literature

WUTHERING
HEIGHTS

Barbara Hardy

BASIL BLACKWELL

© Basil Blackwell 1963

First published 1963
Reprinted 1965
Reprinted with corrections 1983

ISBN 0 631 97580 2

Printed and bound in Great Britain by
Whitstable Litho Ltd., Whitstable, Kent.

GENERAL NOTE

This series of introductions to the great classics of English literature is designed primarily for the school, college, and university student, although it is hoped that they will be found helpful by a much larger audience. Three aims have been kept in mind:

(A) To give the reader the relevant information necessary for his fuller understanding of the work.

(B) To indicate the main areas of critical interest, to suggest suitable critical approaches, and to point out possible critical difficulties.

(C) To do this in as simple and lucid a manner as possible, avoiding technical jargon and giving a full explanation of any critical terms employed.

Each introduction contains questions on the text and suggestions for further reading. It should be emphasized that in no sense is any introduction to be considered as a substitute for the reader's own study, understanding, and appreciation of the work.

THE FAMILY TREE

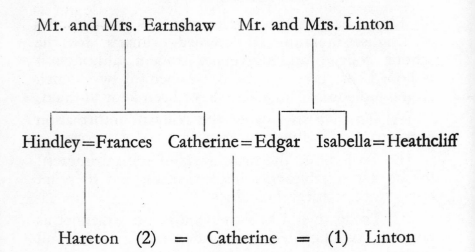

INTRODUCTION

Some of the questions which I want to raise in this book are general questions which could be applied to almost any novel or story. We might well begin by asking what it is that makes us listen to a story? What holds our attention and arouses our curiosity? The stuff of fiction, I suggest, is adventure. The story may be one of physical adventures or of the inner adventures of feeling and imagination. If the story is to involve our sympathies and thoughts and judgements it will almost certainly go beyond physical adventure and indeed many novels written after the end of the nineteenth century dispense with physical adventures altogether. *Wuthering Heights* is one of the most remarkable inner adventure stories written in English, but it most emphatically gives us physical adventures too. The exciting situations of violence, mystery, and tension, which may be described as belonging to the action, are not separable from the excitements of feelings and judgment. Outer and inner adventure go together, interacting symbolically and literally.

Let me give some instances of these outer adventures, of the kind which might be found in a thriller. A man is snowbound and spends the night in an unused room in a lonely house on the moors. A father brings a wild little foundling into his family. His real son and his adopted son grow up in jealousy and hatred. A girl is torn between two loves and virtually wills her own death. The man who is closest

A

to her but whom she does not marry plans and carries out an elaborate and ruthless revenge. He is haunted by the ghost of his dead love and there is some subtle suggestion that the haunting is not confined to him. The daughter of the first girl is one of the victims of his revenge and is kidnapped and forcibly married to his son. There is a happy ending, with the frustration and death of revenger and a harmonious marriage. All these outlined situations suggest the excitements of what I mean by physical adventure. Their action is violent, filled with conflict and mystery. But those of you who already know the novel will agree that even such a bare outline can be seen to imply the conflict and mystery of inner adventures too.

How can a woman be torn between two loves, and with what kind of consequence? What makes a man attempt to degrade another human being? What does it feel like to have nothing but hatred for nearly everyone but a dead woman? These are questions about motivation and action, and the questions and their answers are raised by the characters and their relationships. But the novel is also an adventure for the reader, in a very real sense, forcing him to sift evidence and make difficult judgements. Can we feel anything but distaste and disapproval for ruthless love and revenge? Is Heathcliff a villain or a hero or does he force us to lay aside the usual categories? Is it possible to recognise the happy ending as a harmony but one which lacks something of the passion of earlier discord? Emily Brontë, unlike many great novelists, forces us to give our own answers to such questions of judgment, not merely to assent to her verdict, and in the outer adventures of action, and the inner adventures of characters and reader, she creates a tension which is powerful and rare.

It is not enough to ask about the way in which we respond to the story. As soon as we begin to ask questions about situations and characters, about the problems and excitements they raise, and about the resemblance of their world to our own, we become involved in looking at the novel as a work of art. How is the story organised? Where do we begin and where do we end? And with what effect? From what point of view do we observe these inner and outer adventures? Do the characters act and speak, as in drama, without the explanations and expositions of an author speaking to the reader, or are they presented in the context of the author's moral and psychological commentary, direct or disguised? Who tells the story?

The novel presents us with an exciting experience, tells us a story which holds our interest, and is an artificially constructed work of art. It may also be—and almost always is—an expression of the author's values and beliefs, an illustration or a debate expressed through character and action. I have already said that part of the excitement of this novel comes from its posing of difficult questions. Seeing this makes us do more than examine the lifelike qualities of the characters and actions. It makes us ask whether the characters do more than simply embody vices and virtues. In a novel by Dickens, for instance, it is usually pretty clear that the characters represent certain clear-cut qualities. In *Dombey and Son* we can see that Florence and Paul and Solomon Gills represent the values of love and affection, the values of the heart. Other characters, like Dombey himself until he learns better from experience, demonstrate the opposite values of selfishness and mercenariness. In very many novels there is some kind of division between the sheep and the goats, and usually showing the interesting possibilities of the transformation of goats into sheep. This is true not only of the simplified characters of Dickens but of the more complex psychological creations of George Eliot, where the characters are often less clearly labelled but still express values, where relations and actions and destinies form an argument or a criticism, moral and social. Is there this kind of moral pattern in *Wuthering Heights*? Can we say that Heathcliff and the first Catherine are to be condemned outright, as we can of Pecksniff and Jonas Chuzzlewit? Can we say that Hareton and the second Catherine are to be admired as wholeheartedly as, say, Adam Bede?

I am admittedly making rather crude generalisations about Dickens and George Eliot, which would need modification and more explanation in another context. I do think that it is possible to make some kind of moral generalisation about their characters which many critics have found impossible to make about the characters of *Wuthering Heights*. I believe that it is inappropriate to ask the conventional questions about the moral theme of this novel, just as it is also inappropriate to ask questions about its social relevance, though both these sets of closely related questions usually cry out to be asked when the critic is discussing Victorian novels of this period.

The absence of conventional moral definition and social criticism are not the only differences to be found between *Wuthering Heights* and contemporary novels by Dickens and Thackeray, and (a decade later) George Eliot. *Wuthering Heights* is unusual, though not unique, in its poetic intensity. It is more like *Moby Dick* or *Lady Chatterley's Lover*, in its use of natural symbolism and its powerful lyrical expression, than it is like any novel by Dickens or George Eliot. But it is not a purely poetic novel, but one which has a wide range including not only the hysterical poetry of the two Catherines and the symbolic landscape of the moors and weather, but the solid realism of Nelly Dean and old Joseph.

Lastly, we may ask certain questions about the author and her experiences. We shall not only remember the parsonage at Haworth and the restricted lonely life of Emily who found even the everyday contacts with the villagers difficult, so Charlotte tells us, but the remarkable literary origins of the Brontë novels. The fantasy and even the feelings, the feuds and revenges, the lyrical outbursts, and the character of Heathcliff, can all be related to the fantasy world shared by the Brontë children, especially to the imaginary saga of Gondal which Emily and Anne continued to write about, in letters, diaries, stories, and poems, until their death. Charlotte and their brother Branwell, had collaborated with them in literary fantasy in their childhood, but eventually Emily and Anne broke off from the creation of Angria, and invented their own world of Gondal, traces of which remain chiefly in Emily's poems. The problem of the Gondal origins of

Wuthering Heights, particularly in relation to Heathcliff, is a very complicated one, and I have avoided detailed discussion and merely listed writings on this topic in the Reading List. But I have occasionally made some use of Emily's poems, which seem unquestionably to belong to the world of feeling and action which we find in the novel, and which provide some examples of the influence of Gondal.

Like other novels, *Wuthering Heights* is an absorbing story, a carefully organised work of art, an expression of the author's values, and a creation which can be tenatively related to the life and other writings of Emily Brontë. Although I have stressed these four aspects of the novel in this introduction, and have kept them in mind throughout this book, I have not divided my study under these headings. I have paid some attention to the excitements of the story, the artistic form, the moral problems, and certain external facts, while choosing to follow through three main topics which seem to direct our attention most profitably to the special interests and difficulties of *Wuthering Heights*: its storytellers; its apparently two-fold story of the two generations; and its combination of two worlds, the real everyday world and the suggested appearance of a supernatural world.

TWO STORYTELLERS

(i)

LOCKWOOD

One of the two most important differences between the medium of fiction and the medium of drama is fiction's inclusion of a storyteller. (The other equally important difference is the time-span.) Novels cannot do without a narrator's voice and point of view. The story may be frankly and unashamedly told in the author's voice, as it is in many Victorian novels. This voice may be very quiet and unobtrusive, as in Henry James and quite often in Dickens, or very conspicuously present, as in Thackeray and George Eliot. The author may speak very discreetly, directing our attention to characters and actions but not openly addressing us as readers, nor openly speaking of the characters as fictitious creations. The author may move outside the characters and speak about life in general, and you will find many excellent examples of this enlarging of the fictional world in Fielding and in George Eliot. The author may speak in an invented voice, using a mask (we sometimes call this the author's *persona*) and there are good examples of this in Chaucer's narrative poetry, which has much in common with later prose fiction, and in the early stories of George Eliot, where the author speaks as a man, taking her masculine pseudonym literally. The author may choose to speak in the person of one of the characters, and in eighteenth and nineteenth century novels this is usually the person of the chief character, the hero (as in *Robinson Crusoe*, *David Copperfield*, or *Great Expectations*) or the heroine (as in *Moll Flanders* or *Jane Eyre*). But in some late Victorian novels, for instance in many novels by Conrad, the author can speak directly in the voice of a subordinate character, a spectator of the action, like Marlow in *Lord Jim* and other novels.

Emily Brontë choose to work through two story-tellers, Mr. Lockwood and Nelly Dean, and I propose to consider them each in turn. It would be a mistake to talk about the story and the storytellers as though the reader were continually conscious of the voice and character telling the story. We hear the personal voice and see the scene and the characters through an individual pair of eyes at certain parts of the narrative, but neither Mr. Lockwood nor Nelly Dean remain conspicuously present throughout *all* the novel. Their story is interspersed with other people's stories: we read the first Catherine's diary and Isabella Linton tells of her experiences with Heathcliff in a long letter. Moreover, for much of the novel the story is played out dramatically, and we observe scenes and listen to dialogue almost as we do in a play, though never of course for very long. There are very few novels which are entirely narrated, without this recourse to dramatised action and dialogue. You may like to reflect on the importance of this 'dramatic' presentation.

We are less dependent upon the observations and viewpoint of Lockwood than upon those of Nelly Dean, for he is listener as well as storyteller. In fact,

Wuthering Heights is told as a story within a story. Lockwood's encounter with Heathcliff and Hareton Earnshaw and the second Catherine so arouses his curiosity that he asks Nelly, his housekeeper, to tell him their history. She brings him, and us, up-to-date. Then, after an interval, he comes back and sees the end of the story with his own eyes, with a little further narration from Nelly which fills the gap of his absence. He begins the story, and he also ends it. Both as storyteller and as listener, he is a character of some importance, endowed by the novelist with characteristics which make him a good medium for conveying certain essential effects.

He begins as a good representative of our ignorance, our interest, and our curiosity. He is the stranger in this rough, wild place, the townsman who tells us that he has come in search of seclusion and peace. He comes bringing with him certain superficial expectations and habits of polite society, and makes an ironical contrast with the characters and events which he describes. He is also the ordinary man in an extraordinary situation, and mirrors the mysteries and violence in his bewildered innocence.

Let us consider our first encounter with Lockwood at the very beginning of the novel. The first paragraph tells us that he has 'fixed on a situation . . . completely removed from the stir of society' and he speaks of this as a 'perfect misanthropist's heaven' and of himself and Heathcliff as 'a suitable pair to divide the desolation between us'. The next few pages make it very clear that Lockwood is in fact expecting some sociability, and that he is scarcely to be bracketed with Heathcliff, though the full irony of the comparison does not strike us until much later in the novel. He speaks politely and Heathcliff replies rudely, and in his very interest in Heathcliff's morose reserve, we see that Lockwood's idea of seclusion, misanthropy, and reserve, are little more than the superficial and romantic affectations of a rather feeble and conventional man. Yet Lockwood is no fool: he speculates about his strange rude landlord, but reminds himself that he is 'running on too fast' and bestowing his 'own attributes over liberally on him'. His curiosity is aroused, and the novelist is able to use it, quite naturally, to describe the appearances of things and people in close detail. The detailed description of the strongly built house, with its slanting stunted firs and gaunt thorns, its jutting corner-stones, and its inscription over the door, is an important and compressed introduction to the perverted passions and mystery of Wuthering Heights, the appropriate dwelling-place of Heathcliff. These and other similar details, come into the story unobtrusively, as the puzzled and fascinated stranger explores the strange territory and its inhabitants with the fervour of a lonely tourist.

Lockwood tells us something about himself. His brief account of his failure in love, his inarticulate shyness and his icy retreat, shows that there is some point in his talk about reserve and misanthropy, and shows also his feeble shyness in strong contrast with the directness and fierceness of the passions of the Heights. Once more, the full irony of the contrasts and comparisons does not make itself felt immediately, but gradually. During his two first visits, in the first two chapters, we see the moroseness and rudeness of Heathcliff and Catherine, hear the rough language of Heathcliff, Catherine and old Joseph, and observe the unsociability and the domestic tensions which arouse our curiosity as they do Lockwood's. There are one or two smaller details too. We see that Hareton, though 'entirely devoid of the superiority observable in Mr. and Mrs. Heathcliff', shows some signs of decent behaviour: it is he who asks Lockwood to sit down, and it is he who offers to guide him home through the snow. Catherine too, though ill-tempered and sulky, does at one point observe that 'a man's life is of more consequence than one evening's neglect of the horses'. There is already some indication that both she and Hareton have some humanity which distinguishes them from Heathcliff. We are primarily aware, however, not of these points, but of the hatred and tension which exists within this strange family, and which is exposed the more nakedly in contrast with the polite stranger's attempts at sociability, with his affable conversation, and with his pronounced interest in Catherine. Lockwood observes that he must beware of making Catherine regret her choice of Hareton, when his first misunderstanding about her relationship with Heathcliff gives place to his second misunderstanding about her relationship with Hareton. Though he carefully warns us against finding this reaction conceited, his explanation is carefully placed: 'My neighbour struck me as bordering on repulsive; I knew, through experience, that I was tolerably attractive.' When we read this for the second time, in the full knowledge of subsequent events, its irony is rich, but even at the first reading it is noticeable, insisting that Lockwood's interest is not merely a superficial one, and giving him a slight stake in the story. This is reinforced when Nelly Dean makes a similar match-making suggestion, and again at the end, when Lockwood sees Catherine and Hareton through the window, and looking at her face, bites his lip 'in spite, at having thrown away the chance I might have had of doing something besides staring at its smiling beauty'.

In the second Preface which Charlotte Brontë wrote to *Wuthering Heights*, she spoke of 'the dry, saturnine humour in the delineaton of old Joseph' and there is something of this grim comedy in the early episodes of Lockwood's visits to Heathcliff's house. The contrast between his polite sociability and their rude passions gives rise to humour as well as irony, and this comes out strongly in Lockwood's series of tactfully worded blunders about Catherine being Heathcliff's 'amiable lady' or Hareton being 'the favoured possessor of the beneficent fairy'. The complimentary choice of words is perfect. So is Lockwood's discomfiture. His slow realisation that he feels 'unmistakably out of place in that pleasant family circle ' shows both his humour, and his author's. The humour of *Wuthering Heights* is worth noticing, as well as its varying function.

The humour has its place both in the delineation of widely different characters and in the homely realism. In the passage I have just mentioned, it runs together with a certain amount of necessary information. Lockwood is not merely curious, he is very puzzled. While we are amused by his clumsy-polite attempts to sort out the relationships in the family circle, while its members fight and glare, we are indeed being put in the picture. But the chief effect of the opening chapters is to show us, from the outside, the harshness as well as the mystery, of this strangely-assorted family. We see the rude passions without understanding them. We also see them in sharp relief as they confront and dismay Lockwood's expectations of a call on his landlord and a pleasant taking of tea. His interest and his ignorance, coloured but not entirely distorted by his egoism, bring out the important questions which remain after we have finished the novel. Why will it not do to call Heathcliff a misanthropist, Hareton a clown, Catherine a fairy? These are questions which are raised and soon answered. There are the more difficult questions too. What are the qualities in these harsh passions which have something admirable in them, especially when put beside a gentler lack of spirit? The admiration begins to be implied by these early contrasts, though we are merely sentimentalising the novel if we do not also notice that Emily Brontë begins immediately to show us the cruelty and inhumanity and roughness of her people. Lockwood's alien vision is the medium both for our sense of admiration and for our repugnance.

He begins with a superficial appreciation of this pastoral idyll: 'it is strange how custom can mould our tastes and ideas: many could not imagine the existence of happiness in a life of such complete exile from the world as you spend, Mr. Heathcliff'. But the rough experiences—inhospitable rudeness, attacks by dogs, nose-bleeding—range from serious affront to almost farcical discomfiture and soon lead him beyond such facile and ignorant comments. Yet he returns eventually, with us, to a more just appraisal of the values of a rough and wild exile from society, and even in Chapter VII, after the beginnings of Nelly's story, what he has to say is more to the point than his first reactions: 'I perceive that people in these regions acquire over people in towns the value that the spider in a dungeon does over a spider in a cottage, to their various occupants; and yet the deepened attraction is not entirely owing to the situation of the looker-on. They *do* live more in earnest, more in themselves, and less in surface change, and frivolous external things.'

Wuthering Heights is not the kind of novel which teaches its spectator-commentator new values. He is a forced listener, trapped both by his desire for rustic solitude and by a bad cold. He shows the superficiality of his misanthropy by enlisting Nelly Dean and the passions of his neighbours to while away the time and provide him with the human contact he finds he cannot dispense with.

He is given just enough individual interest to give him a stake in the story and to bring out the contrasts and ironies I have mentioned, but it does not do to exaggerate his importance. For instance, his weaknesses are emphasised where they are needed, in the first scenes which introduce us to *Wuthering Heights* or in the scene where he tells Nelly that her rationality and judgment testifies to the values of rural existence. Where they are not needed, as for the greater stretch

of Nelly's narrative, they simply disappear. A more
strongly individualised character would have been
more difficult to keep in the background as a mere
listening ear. Moreover, Lockwood is sometimes
right as well as wrong in his judgment. He says that
Nelly idealises the second Catherine, which seems a
fair enough comment. Even though he is perhaps
talking over-romantically when he observes that
coming to this place has made him feel that a lasting
love might after all be possible (Chapter VII) this
comment does come in a novel which shows, with
precision and no sentimentality, one of the most
lasting loves in literature. He gives sound and sensitive
advice to Catherine about her conduct to Hareton.
At the end his weaknesses are not given emphasis. He
has lost another opportunity, but his comment on this
throws emphasis on the story itself as well as humorously casting a last light on Lockwood. This is what he
can say near the end of the story:

> What a realisation of something more romantic
> than a fairy-tale it would have been for Mrs.
> Linton Heathcliff, had she and I struck up an
> attachment, as her good nurse desired, and
> migrated together into the stirring atmosphere of
> the town! (Chapter XXXI).

This is a comment worth looking at. The words
'romantic' and 'stirring atmosphere' are excellently
two-edged.

When he comes back, in 1802, almost by accident,
to hear the end of the story, I think that his character
and situation are subordinated. Emily Brontë exploits
those characteristics she has early established—his

superficial desires for solitude, his changeableness, and his real sensibility—to motivate both his absence and his return, and thus enables the story to be consistently completed. It comes to us filtered through Nelly Dean's experience and point of view as well as through his, but what we have glimpsed of his experience is very slight compared with all we have lived through with Nelly. But after Nelly has said her last words, Lockwood says his, and his are indeed the last words of the novel.

These last words bring out the contrast between their two points of view. Nelly believes that the dead are at peace, but feels a superstitious fear when he speaks lightly about leaving Wuthering Heights 'for the use of such ghosts as choose to inhabit it'. After she has shown her characteristic blend of common-sense and superstition, which he has earlier found 'heterodox', he visits the three graves and makes the last quiet comment on the strong passions so alien to him. At the last, he is a spectator, but his response is a sympathetic one: 'I lingered round them, under that benign sky; watched the moths fluttering among the heath and harebells, listened to the soft wind breathing through the grass, and wondered how any one could ever imagine unquiet slumbers for the sleepers in that quiet earth.'

Questions.

1. Give an account of Lockwood's character and his contribution to the novel.

2. Lockwood, like most of the characters in the novel, is shown with criticism and sympathy. How

are (*a*) his weaknesses and (*b*) his good qualities, made to draw our attention to the main characters and events?

3.   Look at some of Lockwood's dialogue with Nelly Dean, and comment on its function.

4.   Are his storytelling and his listening made to appear natural and plausible? If you think they are, try to say why.

5.   What contribution is made to the novel by Catherine's 'diary' and Isabella's letter?

*6.   The story might have been 'told' to us directly by Nelly Dean. What do you think we would have lost without Lockwood?

*7.   I have so far said nothing about Lockwood's dream. Try to say something about its place and function in the immediate context of Chapter III and in the novel as a whole. Why do you think he is made to dream *two* dreams?

*Questions marked by an asterisk are intended for advanced students or for the interest of teachers.

NELLY DEAN

Lockwood is a stranger, the visitor from the alien
environment of 'the busy world'. He is educated and
'civilised'. Nelly Dean, his opposite in this as in so
many ways, is a native of the moors and has grown up
with the characters whose story she tells. There might
have been one slight technical difficulty in combining
the contributions of these two very different story-
tellers, the linguistic difficulty of combining the prose
style of an educated man and that of an uneducated
woman. Emily Brontë gets round this difficulty. First,
she makes Lockwood comment explicitly on Nelly's
powers of expression and intelligence. In Chapter
VII, he observes, not perhaps entirely without con-
descension, that Nelly is a good example of the
superior earnestness of the inhabitants of these lonely
moors:

> Excepting a few provincialisms of slight
> consequence, you have no marks of the manners
> which I am habituated to consider as peculiar to
> your class. I am sure that you have thought a
> good deal more than the generality of servants
> think. You have been compelled to cultivate
> your reflective faculties for want of occasions for
> frittering your life away in silly trifles.

If Lockwood learns to revise his expectations of
social intercourse with his landlord he also comes to
revise his assumptions about the servant 'class'.
When he first mentions Nelly it is very much in the

humorously condescending tone of a gentleman tolerating the defects of the lower orders, especially the lower orders in the country: 'N.B.—I dine between twelve and one o'clock; the housekeeper, a matronly lady, taken as a fixture along with the house, could not, or would not, comprehend my request that I might be served at five' (Chapter II). It seems plain that Emily Brontë is not merely justifying the literacy of her narrative when she makes Lockwood praise Nelly's powers and when she makes Nelly calmly and good-temperedly answer his rather Wordsworthian views about rustic surroundings. Nelly's sense and quiet self-knowledge combine when she replies that she esteems herself 'a steady, reasonable kind of body' but explains that she would herself attribute her qualities less to a pastoral environment than to 'sharp discipline, which has taught me wisdom' and to a good library, from which she has benefited as much as can be expected 'of a poor man's daughter'. This is Emily Brontë's second explanation for Nelly's powers of thought and expression. I am not suggesting that the little piece of dialogue is merely her way of clutching this nettle and explaining how a servant can be given the burden of this narrative. Clearly, there are characteristics of both master and servant brought out admirably in the short passage. But Emily Brontë also brings the difficulty out into the open, or, if you prefer, makes it plain that there is going to be no difficulty, since here we have a woman of sense and intelligence. I labour this point in order to emphasise not only the language, but the commentary and reflection.

Nelly's is no artless gossip's tale—both Lockwood and Heathcliff, incidentally, affirm that she is no 'gossip'—but a tale where reflection plays its part as well as action. Nelly has not only to respond to the significance of some of the events—though I think not by any means to all of them—but she also intersperses her story with much explicit comment and judgement. We may look at the problem of choosing a storyteller as a technical choice of endowing a character with the requisite characteristics, or we may see Nelly as an essential part of the original conception. Either choice is speculative. What is important and definite is that story and storyteller seem to be perfectly matched. Emily Brontë draws our attention to the qualifications of the storyteller, though she is doing other things as well. She also makes Lockwood explain that he will keep the story in Nelly's own words, condensing a little, but not needing 'to improve her style' and he is made to demur when Nelly suggests skipping a year or two and begs her to leave out nothing. The first comment is necessary in order to prevent us raising doubts about the endurance of this storyteller or alternately to avoid a laborious interruption of the story to give details about each session. The second comment also excuses the detail which passes in a novel but might again be objected to by over-realistic readers. Emily Brontë is clearly aware of the importance of such small technical points and her readers cannot object, like some of the hypercritical readers of Richardson's *Pamela*, to the feats of endurance necessary to such a piece of storytelling. These are some of the small problems involved in using a character within the action for the role of narrator.

As I have said earlier, for much of the novel the characters speak for themselves and act without the intrusions of Nelly's commentary, but if you look closely you will find that her commentary does not fade out for long. We are for the most part very much aware of her presence. This is because she tells the story as a judge and commentator, summing up not only the actions and motives of the characters but also on occasion summing up her own responses and judgments. It is also because, unlike Lockwood, she is closely involved in the action and intimately attached to the people. She is shown in active relationship with the characters whose fate she witnesses, and there are many times when she is a victim or an agent rather than a mere witness. But it is also true that she, like Lockwood, is used to provide a strong contrast with the passions and conduct of the main characters. Lockwood's lack of involvement in life, his romantic or conventional judgements, and his urbanity, are characteristics which throw into striking relief the rudeness and vitality of the life which confronts him. Nelly's conventional morality (its tinge of superstition does not prevent it from being basically conventional) and rational matter-of-factness make her a sober nurse to a very wild nursery. She grows up with Hindley Earnshaw, who was fostered by her mother, and she never forgets her early ties with him. In her relationship with Hindley we are aware both of the gulf between them and the bridge of humanity which plays its part in controlling our response to him. He is one of the least attractive and most culpable characters in the novel, and Nelly's feeling for him is as important as the contrast between them. But the main contrast is between Nelly and the two groups of main characters and this, like the contrast I have just briefly mentioned, depends not merely on her differences but also on the close tie of feeling. She is a foil and a contrast but never strikes us as a purely functional character because she is so personally involved.

There is one sense in which we might call Nelly detached rather than involved. She has these ties of love and loyalty but does not appear to have any 'private life' of her own. There is never any suggestion (in spite of Joseph's references to her 'fellies') that Nelly Dean has any important emotional relations except those of nurse to nurslings. She is in this way, like Lockwood, shown as living vicariously and placed in a good position to comment on other people's passionate conduct. But the comparison with Lockwood brings out the difference between them. There is certainly no suggestion that Nelly stands apart from life in timidity, coldness, or lack of spirit. Lockwood sometimes talks as if he might become personally involved, or might have become personally involved, with these characters, but this suggestion serves only to emphasise his essential detachment. Nelly, on the other hand, never for a moment mentions any attachments other than her attachments to the people she serves, but this brings out her deep involvement in loyalty and affection, and in disapproval and intolerance, with the main characters.

She has grown up with Hindley and the first Catherine, his sister. She has played and helped and lived in the Earnshaw family since her childhood, and then works as a servant and as nurse to Hareton and to the second Catherine. (We are told nothing about her own family except for one or two tiny details). She forms an important link between the two houses, since she is forced reluctantly to leave Wuthering Heights and go with the first Catherine to Thrushcross Grange on Catherine's marriage to Edgar Linton. She lives in intimate relationship with all the chief characters, and, whether as servant, nurse, or housekeeper, on equal terms of friendship or disapproval. Her affections and her intolerance are those of the valued servant who can speak her mind and can be confided in. One of the most moving instances of this, I think, comes when Heathcliff speaks to her at the end, telling her that she is the only person to whom he can speak, relieving the pressure within his mind 'so eternally secluded in itself'. It is, technically speaking, necessary for the storyteller to be a confidante, but Nelly's qualities fully fit for the rôle. Once more, it is impossible to separate her function in the novel from her vivid portrayal as a human being.

She follows the domestic moves and upheavals. She is torn from Hareton when he is a small child, and laments his wasted intelligence and unchristian upbringing. She learns to respect her new master, Edgar Linton. She is forced to share the second Catherine's imprisonment in Wuthering Heights. And she is eventually separated from her, so that we see her begging details from Lockwood and even employing him as a messenger. We see her at last serving

Heathcliff and growing strangely close to him in his last haunted days.

Throughout all we see Nelly the good servant, loyal but outspoken, loving but critical. In her sober realism and sense we have a constant check on our response to the wild passions of the central pair, Heathcliff and the first Catherine. Without Nelly, I suggest, we might condemn them too harshly, for part of her function is to insist on their humanity. Without Nelly we might, on the other hand, accept these violent constant lovers too readily as an ideal, for the other part of her function is to insist on their folly and selfishness. She tethers what might have been a wildly romantic story to reality. When Juliet's Nurse in *Romeo and Juliet* reminds us of the ordinary common world of coarse jokes about sex, matter-of-fact earthiness, and honest-to-goodness compromise (she doesn't see why Juliet should make such a fuss about marrying Paris) she sharpens the intensity and rarity of the passions she serves. But she has no real effect on the action. Nelly's function is in many ways like that of the Nurse, but she is not only a more sophisticated judge and critic, but a complex character and one who has some responsibility for events.

Let us first consider her rôle as critic. It is important to recognise that her rationality and commonsense is something which grows slowly and painfully in the course of the novel. She does not spring fully endowed from her author's imagination, but has her beginnings, her changes, her education by experience. I have said that hers is the unromantic view which says straight out that the first Catherine is ignorant and wicked, both in her marriage to Edgar and in her self-willed death, and this kind of criticism prevents us from taking the novel as a celebration of passion. But the world of commonsense has its part to play in the tragedy, and Nelly is by no means a perfect human being. As the novel follows its course we see the truth of what she says to Lockwood, that she has learnt her rationality and sobriety through sharp discipline. Nelly is often right, but she is also sometimes wrong.

At the beginning (the chronological beginning) of the story, when Earnshaw brings Heathcliff from Liverpool, Nelly first reacts, like the others, in callous revulsion: 'They entirely refused to have it in bed with them, or even in their room; and I had no more sense, so I put it on the landing of the stairs, hoping it might be gone on the morrow.' Even the 'it' of this sentence plays its part. Nelly criticises her foolish former self as she tells the story, commenting on the unjust treatment which both she and Hindley dealt to the foundling. She hated him, she 'wasn't reasonable enough to feel (her) injustice' she joined her pinches to Hindley's blows. We see the young Nelly Dean as a rough, insensitive, and unreflecting girl. She softens a little when she has to nurse Heathcliff through his attack of measles, but comments that she couldn't 'dote' on him. In all this flashback story, in Chapter IV, we see not only Nelly but also Heathcliff. She explains, for instance, that she misunderstood the boy's lack of complaint and 'really thought him not vindictive: I was deceived completely, as you will hear'.

Her criticism of old Joseph is an interesting strand

of forthright and humorous comment and action which runs through the novel giving us some sense of her reliability and sensibility, but her judgment is continually being modified. Hers is a full human reaction. She is very critical of the first Catherine, refuses to be ruled and bullied by her, and therefore reminds us of Catherine's ill-tempered bullying streak. There is no lack of feeling when it is required, as in the scene when she listens to Catherine and Heathcliff comforting each other with pictures of heaven after Earnshaw's death: 'while I sobbed and listened, I could not help wishing we were all there safe together'.

In her criticism and shift from sympathy to a lack of sympathy—with Heathcliff, Cathy, or Frances Earnshaw—we see the critical loyalty, without the blindness of some kinds of love, which can be felt within a family circle. This loyalty serves not only as a good medium for the narrative, but also as a strong contrast with, for instance, the blinded loves of Edgar and Isabella for Catherine and Heathcliff. It also combines with Nelly's intelligence and self-respect to put her in a position of equality, as well as intimacy, with the other characters, so that she speaks her mind as mentor and confidante. Her blend of reason and error comes out excellently in her relationship with the first Catherine, who confides in her (while Heathcliff listens, fatally, to the wrong part of the confidence) about her conflict and divided love.

This crisis comes in Chapter IX, in the peaceful setting of the kitchen. Nelly is lulling the little Hareton to sleep. Catherine comes in and tells first of her love for Edgar and her acceptance of his pro-

posal, and then of her intuitive feeling that she is
acting wrongly. She reveals her feeling that her love
for Heathcliff 'resembles the eternal rocks'. Nelly puts
her through a 'catechism', to use her own word, and
comments with characteristic dry humour that 'for a girl
of twenty-two it was not injudicious'. Her judgement is
sure and simple: she is direct, impatient, and, to use
another of her own words, 'sententious'. Her comment on Catherine's motives for marriage, commands
our assent. She speaks of Catherine's folly, and tells
her that she is either ignorant of her duties or unprin-
cipled, and although there are perhaps some things in
Catherine's revelations of which she seems neglectful,
her rational moral sense is sound, and her prophecy
about separation and desolation is more accurate than
Catherine's wild hopes of keeping both her loves.
Nelly is not however entirely the rational moralist, and
her superstitious streak comes in when Catherine tries
to tell her of a dream. Nelly prevents Catherine telling
the terrible dream which gave her 'an unusual gloom
in her aspect, that made me dread something from
which I might shape a prophecy' but listens to what
we are told is 'apparently' another dream, the dream
of desolate exile in heaven. Nelly's susceptibility and
superstition accompanies her common-sense, and this
little passage has special significance in the novel.

Nelly's rôle as a 'chorus' depends on our impression
of her as a complex human being. She has many
aspects, behaves both well and badly, and is shown as
changing and developing. Just as she treated the
young Heathcliff harshly so she later treats Catherine
with a certain complacent hardness. She is indeed

literally responsible for her death, since she refrains
from telling Edgar that Catherine has taken no food:
'I wasted no condolences on Miss (Isabella), nor any
expostulations on my mistress; nor did I pay much
attention to the sighs of my master, who yearned to
hear his lady's name. . ..' She is 'convinced that the
Grange had put one sensible soul in its walls '. She is
convinced that Catherine is acting a part, since one of
the things she cannot understand is that Catherine
wills her sickness but does not *affect* it, and she keeps
the truth from Edgar and gives Catherine the impression that he is undisturbed and 'among his books'.
Here the older and wiser Nelly interposes the comment
that she would not have so spoken so 'if I had known
her true condition'. And she is strongly rebuked when
her master finds out.

   We might make a long list of Nelly's errors, and
indeed she is conscious of them herself, wondering, for
instance, if she is right or wrong to be persuaded by
Heathcliff to connive at his visit in Edgar's absence,
and concluding 'I fear it was wrong, though expedient'.
Later in the novel, when it is the second Catherine who
is in her care, she is very much more affectionate and
protective, but there is the same struggle within a
trap. She is forced by the second Catherine and by
Heathcliff into certain compromises, and because she
has loyalties on both sides, and needs to protect
Edgar, her stern moral principles are deflected into
various treacheries. But throughout the action her
commentary is there as an unromantic guide.

   When Heathcliff embraces Catherine on her sick
bed Nelly feels as if he belongs to another species. She

does not talk to the reader behind the back of the characters, however, and the dialogue between Nelly and the various misguided characters—Edgar, both Catherines, Isabella, and Heathcliff—is often forceful and blunt. Her criticism and her appeals—to Heathcliff or his son—are contrasted with her helplessness. At no point in the novel is she permitted to interfere for good, and there are times when her actions are disastrous, whether from weakness or from self-righteousness. It is worth following through Nelly Dean's process beyond this point to observe the way in which the bitter experiences of Catherine and the enforced separation make Nelly a wiser and less complacent woman.

In her relationship with Heathcliff, for instance, she is patient, terrified, protective, and has none of the harsh tones or complacency of the young Nelly Dean. At the end she is less the critic than the sympathetic friend, rejoicing in the 'happy ending' for Catherine and Hareton—'I shall envy no one on their wedding-day: there won't be a happier woman than myself in England!' and oppressed with sorrow for Heathcliff's end. She sums up the paradox of our antipathy and sympathy, and yet there are tones and implications which Nelly can only record without comprehending. When Heathcliff speaks of his haunted anguish at the end, Nelly brings us down to earth with the bathos of 'from childhood he had a delight in dwelling on dark things and entertaining old fancies' and 'I was inclined to believe, as he said Joseph did, that conscience had turned his heart to an earthly hell'. The phrase 'entertaining odd fancies' is a little inadequate, to put it mildly, for Heathcliff's agony, and the word 'conscience' is not exactly appropriate. Nelly has guided us through the story, slowly developing her sound principles and her strong affections, but both her weaknesses and her strengths are made at times to be unreliable guides. It is indeed 'another species' on which she comments, and we should be less aware of the extraordinary passions of the story if they did not come to us through the voice and mind and heart of Nelly Dean.

Questions.

1. List the strengths and weaknesses of Nelly's character.

2. One of the difficulties in using the detached storyteller comes up when the characters have to be shown in intimate or passionate contact. Some of the love-scenes in this novel would not normally take place when a third person was present. Look at the end of Chapter III, where we see Heathcliff agonising over his dead love, at Chapter VIII, where Catherine and Edgar have a stormy scene, and at Chapter XV, where Heathcliff comes to visit the dying Catherine. How has the author succeeded in giving plausible second-hand reports of these scenes? Find some more examples for yourself.

3. What has Nelly to say about Edgar Linton? There is plenty of interesting material in Chapters IX-XIV, and you might also bear the question in mind when reading later chapters.

4. Nelly is strongly critical of Hindley Earnshaw and Heathcliff, but also shows some attachment to

them. Find some examples of scenes where this attachment is shown, explicitly or implicitly, and comment on the impression made on the reader.

5. Nelly tells Lockwood that she has 'undergone sharp discipline' (Chapter VII). What evidence is there of this 'sharp discipline' in the novel?

*6. Read these lines, which come from Nelly's narrative at the beginning of Chapter X:

Well, we *must* be for ourselves in the long run; the mild and generous are only more justly selfish than the domineering; and it ended when circumstances caused each to feel that the one's interest was not the chief consideration in the other's thoughts. On a mellow evening in September, I was coming from the garden with a heavy basket of apples which I had been gathering. It had got dusk, and the moon looked over the high wall of the court, causing undefined shadows to lurk in the corners of the numerous projecting portions of the building. I set my burden on the house steps by the kitchen door, and lingered to rest, and drew in a few more breaths of the soft, sweet air. . . .

What is interesting in this passage?

You might bear in mind Nelly's general habit of moral reflection and your own response to the application of her first sentence to the characters in the novel, as well as considering the effect and placing of the description in the rest of the passage. Turn up Chapter X and see what follows. Ask yourself too whether this is a passage which could only come from the lips of this imaginary storyteller or whether it might form part of a story told in the third person.

SECTION TWO

THE TWO GENERATIONS

(i)

HEATHCLIFF-CATHERINE-EDGAR LINTON

Wuthering Heights is a novel with two storytellers.
It is also a novel telling the story of two generations.
The relation of one 'story' to another is very unlike the
usual relation between the stories in most Victorian
novels with a multiple action and I think it is important
not to think of the novel as made up of two stories,
but rather as one story told in two parts.

In *David Copperfield* or *Vanity Fair*, *Middlemarch* or
Uncle Tom's Cabin, there are two or more clearly
separated strands of action. These strands are inter-
woven into a unified whole, but we turn from one set
of characters to another in turn. In *Vanity Fair* we
begin with Becky Sharp and Amelia, but after a while
their histories, though intimately connected, diverge,
and each action is allowed to have its say, rotating in
fairly equal division of time and space. In novels of
this kind of construction the separate actions are linked
by the social background, the themes, and by the
practical impingement of one part upon another. The
major characters in one action eventually appear as
minor characters in another. There is strong contrast
and parallel. Sometimes comedy is followed by serious
action, as in *Oliver Twist*, or in some of Trollope's
novels, where there is something closely akin to the

division into main plot and sub-plot found in Elizabethan drama. Dickens compared the double action in *Oliver Twist* to the composition of 'streaky bacon'. There is usually a moral contrast too, between characters and action, and this is usually thrown into relief by some degree of resemblance, so that we are made to alternate between this reaction: 'They have this in common, but the differences are vast', and this: 'They are strikingly different but still have this in common.'

The Brontë sisters did not write multiple novels of this kind. *Jane Eyre* and *Villette*, by Charlotte Brontë, or *Agnes Grey*, by Anne Brontë, are concentrated pieces of first-person narrative, single stories told from the central viewpoint of the heroine. I should remind you, in passing, that the first-person narrator may of course be used in a large multiple novel. David Copperfield tells his own story and that of several other groups of people, and Esther's first-person narrative, in *Bleak House*, takes its turn with another strand of narrative told in the author's voice. *Wuthering Heights* differs from the other Brontë novels I have mentioned in not being told by the protagonist. We might indeed have some difficulty in deciding if there is one protagonist, as there is in *Jane Eyre*. It is also different in the way it presents this double history of two generations.

Though it differs in these structural features from its sister novels, it will not do to class it with *Vanity Fair* or *David Copperfield*. Its two-part structure, though intricate, is not an equal division and does not make us shift the focus. The division into two storytellers is a very unequal division, with Lockwood beginning and interrupting and concluding the novel,

C

but actually doing much more listening than telling, and so also the division into two stories of two generations does not clearly divide the narrative into distinctly separate parts. There is nothing like the movement away from one generation to the next, with a constant though subtle change of focus, which we get in D. H. Lawrence's *The Rainbow*. In *Wuthering Heights* the two generations are presented together, rather than in historical sequence.

There is a large overlap between the stories, so that we should not call them separate stories at all. Heathcliff, the hero (or the villain-hero?) has a career which over-arches the whole action and the novel ends almost immediately after we have been shown his death. There is some shift of focus within Nelly's story, which is told in chronological order, but this is really only true of the replacement of the first by the second Catherine. Heathcliff still controls the action, both as an agent and as a centre of interest, and the second Catherine's presence is felt after her death. There is resolution and peace and a happy ending in the second generation, after the tragic sufferings of the first, but this does not *succeed* the end of the first generation. Both ends come together.

Emily Brontë's unusual and intricate ordering of time ensures that we do not follow one history after the other. The novel does not adopt the chronicle pattern of the 'autobiographical' novel like *David Copperfield*, which follows the characters through from birth to maturity, or of the 'saga' novels of Trollope or Galsworthy. It is as bold an experiment with time as *Tristram Shandy*, or *Daniel Deronda*, or *Eyeless in Gaza*, and resembles these three novels in its deliberate blurring of normal time-sequence. Reading time does not follow historical time.

The novel begins in 1801, a year before it ends. We see first, through Lockwood's eyes, the two generations, living together in unhappy tension. It is the second Catherine who first engages Lockwood's interest and our own, and she is seen with Heathcliff and Hareton. The closeness in age is also emphasised —a small but not an insignificant point—for it is possible, as Lockwood's misunderstanding brings out, that Heathcliff might be married to Catherine. Catherine is immediately overshadowed by the ghost of her mother, the first Catherine, who makes her first terrifying appearance in Lockwood's dream, as he sleeps in her old room and after he reads her scrawls on the ledge and in her informal diary. The two generations make their appearance together.

The novel does not begin in the middle, in the approved epic fashion, but nearly at the end. The reader moves, with Lockwood's questions and Nelly's story, back to the beginning, and thereafter, with one or two interruptions, we do move through the events in historical sequence. Then there is another interruption when Lockwood goes away, and his return brings about the occasion for Nelly to bring us all up to date in the last brief flashback. Both the handling of time, and the continued emphasis on Heathcliff (not to mention his sense of the first Catherine's presence) makes it impossible for us to discuss the novel in terms of two separate stories.

However, though I have so far insisted that the

novel presents the two actions together, it is both possible and useful to notice *some* resemblances between the double action in *Wuthering Heights* and in that of the multiple novel of Dickens, George Eliot, or Thackeray. Although the two 'stories' overlap, and although Heathcliff remains, I suggest, the centre of attention, the narrative organisation presents these two generations in terms of prominent likeness and difference. Before I go on to demonstrate this organisation, I want first to bring out the prominent features in the first generation.

There are three main characters in the first generation: Heathcliff, Catherine, and Edgar Linton. They are of course presented as an eternal triangle, held together by personal tensions. They are, like most characters in good novels, representative of certain values, but in an unusual and complex way. One of the remarkable features of Emily Brontë's imagination is its ability to entertain opposing values within single characters. It would be possible to applaud this as realistic, but there are other things which must be said too.

In the characters of Heathcliff and the first Catherine there is a 'realistic' combination of bad and admirable qualities, but the actual result of the combination is by no means ordinary or common. Emily Brontë is not merely demonstrating a belief that human beings do not fall neatly into categories, so that all the admirable and all the repulsive qualities are gathered together. She is concerned to show a love of great and rare intensity, and she expresses it less in sexual terms than in terms of imaginative identity. 'I am Heathcliff' says Catherine, and the normal terms of desire are not used, though there is one occasion when the lovers embrace. The love is expressed in terms of identity, and also in terms of permanence. Lastly, it is expressed in terms of remarkable vitality. It is this vitality which explains the shared identity and which seems to explain the permanence.

Let us see how these three aspects of her love are expressed by Catherine as she unfolds her conflict to Nelly Dean.

This is the part of the confidence which is not overheard by Heathcliff. If it had been, the novel would have probably been very different. This is what Catherine says.

> My great miseries in this world have been Heathcliff's miseries, and I watched and felt each from the beginning: my great thought in living is himself. If all else perished, and *he* remained, *I* should continue to be; and if all else remained, and he were annihilated, the universe would turn to a mighty stranger: I should not seem a part of it. My love for Linton is like the foliage in the woods: time will change it, I'm well aware, as winter changes the trees. My love for Heathcliff resembles the eternal rocks beneath: a source of little visible delight, but necessary. Nelly, I *am* Heathcliff! He's always, always in my mind: not as a pleasure, any more than I am always a pleasure to myself, but as my own being. (Chapter IX).

This brings out the sense of fused identities and the sense of permanence. It is also a direct prophecy of Heathcliff's last tormented feelings. He tells Nelly that

'The entire world is a dreadful collection of memoranda that she did exist, and that I have lost her!' but at the same time he foresees the 'change' which is soon to come about, and this seems to be the change from the sense of her absence to the sense of her presence. Nelly is as incapable of understanding Catherine's statement of love as she is of understanding Heathcliff's haunted rapture at the end. Yet she is, as usual, both reliable and unreliable. She shows insight and sense in talking about Catherine's ignorant folly, and in mentioning 'married duties' but admits that she is incapable of taking in what Catherine is saying. She replies to Heathcliff by saying that he should seek advice from a minister of religion who might show him that he will be unfit for heaven: she is right about his 'selfish, unchristian life' but wide of the mark in mentioning heaven. Just how wide of the mark she is we can see by turning back to Chapter IX, where Catherine tells the story of her dream of heaven:

> I was only going to say that heaven did not seem to be my home; and I broke my heart with weeping to come back to earth; and the angels were so angry that they flung me out into the middle of the heath on the top of Wuthering Heights; where I woke sobbing for joy. That will do to explain my secret, as well as the other. I've no more business to marry Edgar Linton than I have to be in heaven; and if the wicked man in there had not brought Heathcliff so low, I shouldn't have thought of it.

Nelly is sound, however, in rebuking Catherine's ignorance. Her common-sense is a reliable guide when she is faced with Catherine's ignorant and impractical proposal to allow Edgar's wealth to 'aid Heathcliff to rise, and place him out of my brother's power' and her equally ignorant hope that 'Edgar must shake off his antipathy, and tolerate him, at least. He will, when he learns my true feelings towards him.' Nelly is right in thinking that Edgar will not prove as 'pliable' as Catherine calculates, right in condemning this particular motive for marrying Edgar, and ultimately right in her vague prediction that Heathcliff and Catherine will be desolately separated. But Catherine's passionate sense of identity with Heathcliff remains as much beyond the scope of her comprehension as Heathcliff's last torment and joy. Nelly is very sound in her judgements of Edgar Linton or Isabella, but when she tells us that Heathcliff seemed to her to belong to a different species, she is merely drawing attention to a distinction made throughout the novel.

This is the distinction presented by Catherine when she compares her love for Edgar to the summer foliage and her love for Heathcliff to the eternal rocks beneath, or when she declares: 'Whatever our souls are made of, his and mine are the same; and Linton's is as different as a moonbeam from lightning, or frost from fire.' It is not, in my opinion, the distinction drawn by Lord David Cecil in his book *Early Victorian Novelists*, between the children of calm and the children of storm. Catherine and Heathcliff are distinguished not only from Edgar Linton and Isabella (whose resemblance to each other is much exaggerated in Lord David Cecil's argument) but also from all the other characters in the novel.

But they are not distinguished only by this vitality and enduring love. They are distinguished also by their selfishness and ruthlessness. Edgar Linton shares neither their vitality nor their disregard for other people, and the distinction is rather like the distinction between Falstaff and Prince Hal, or Caesar and Antony. In such comparisons there is no simple balance sheet but a confusion of credits and debits. We admire spirit but disapprove of the havoc and pain it causes. We admire gentleness and morality but observe that it is bracketed with a certain passiveness and tameness and lack of imagination. In this clash of the first generation Emily Brontë is showing that it is difficult to make moral judgements, that our imaginative and passionate feeling may be drawn towards disorder and ruthlessness. She is not, I believe, showing a passion which 'transcends' morality. Heathcliff and Catherine are immoral—cruel, selfish, malicious, foolish—but since their cruelty and malice and folly is shown to work because of their love, or in the interests of their love, it is not possible to separate the admirable qualities from the repulsive ones.

I do not, however, want to suggest that Emily Brontë shows their bad qualities as coming entirely out of the tragic circumstances of their poverty, their harsh environment, and the pressures exercised by Hindley Earnshaw and society. Catherine and Heathcliff are shown as respectively wilful and hard before the last stages of Hindley's treatment makes Catherine insist that it has been made impossible for them to marry. One could argue that Heathcliff's environment, implied and later shown, has made him hard, but Catherine's selfishness is not shown as entirely a product of her environment. We should give the environment some responsibility but not read this novel as if it were a modern study of the childhood origins of delinquency. Catherine needs to marry a rich man, according to her own argument, which has some sense in it, but she is also drawn to Edgar's good looks and pleasant charm. We should not underestimate the strength of this attraction. She admits that it is nothing beside her feeling for Heathcliff but it is neither purely mercenary nor trivial: 'I love the ground under his feet, and the air over his head, and everything he touches, and every word he says'. And in the later development of Edgar's portrait we find some justification for this love. Indeed, the strength of her feeling for Heathcliff depends in part on her loving him *in spite of* his hardness and roughness. It has little to do with pleasure, she says, and this is true in more senses than one. This is a romantic portrayal of love in its emphasis on inaccessibility and pain and permanence, but it is unromantically shown and both said and shown to be distinctly unideal in many ways.

But the emphasis given in this first generation to the repulsive and disorderly *and* the enduring and ecstatic nature of the love of Heathcliff and Catherine needs more than the contrasts with Edgar Linton. We must turn to the second generation in order to see the novel as a whole.

Questions.
   1. What is admirable in Heathcliff and the first Catherine and what is not?

2. Consider Catherine's account of Heathcliff to Isabella (Chapter X). She speaks of him as 'an arid wilderness of furze and whinstone'. What do you think of this choice of imagery?

3. There are two mysteries connected with Heathcliff: his origin and his later acquisition of education and wealth. Consider the effects of these two gaps in our knowledge.

4. What does Heathcliff say about himself and how accurate is his self-knowledge? Look especially at Chapters XIV and XXXIII.

5. I have tended to talk of Heathcliff and Catherine as if they resembled each other in every respect. It could be argued that Catherine is more culpable than Heathcliff: try to think of reasons *for* and *against* this view and work towards your own conclusions.

6. Consider the presentation of Heathcliff, Catherine, and Edgar in Chapter X and Chapter XI.

7. You will have noticed, if you have tried Question 6, that Heathcliff's relationship with Isabella introduces new tensions and changed responses in various characters. Give some account of these.

*8. What justification can you find for Emily Brontë's use of the 'accidental' circumstance that Heathcliff overhears part of Catherine's confidence to Nelly in Chapter IX and goes away without hearing her account of her love for him?

*9. What is the interest of this comparison made by Nelly Dean in Chapter VIII?

Doubtless Catherine marked the difference between her friends, as one came in and the other went out. The contrast resembled what you see in exchanging a bleak, hilly, coal country for a beautiful fertile valley, and his voice and greeting were as opposite as his aspect. He had a sweet, low manner of speaking, and pronounced his words as you do: that's less gruff than we talk here, and softer.

(ii)

HARETON–CATHERINE–LINTON
HEATHCLIFF

We see the second generation as victims of the havoc caused by the first. Hareton is the victim of Heathcliff's revenge against Hindley Earnshaw, Catherine the victim of his revenge against Edgar Linton. Their degradation is part of the plot, and this involves both harsh treatment (though the harshness varies considerably in each case) and financial deprivation. Linton, the sickly product of Heathcliff's coldly deliberated marriage with Isabella, in which he is seen at his very worst, is preserved and used as bait for Catherine. Heathcliff's revenge is an attempt to get an eye for an eye and a tooth for a tooth in an exact way, since he matches his own early degradation with Hareton's, and his early poverty by taking the properties of Wuthering Heights and Thrushcross Grange. His foresight and subtlety and legalistic means of action make him a coolly ingenious villain like some of the avengers in Jacobean drama. We might add also his partial justification, his psychological manipulation of individuals, his smooth diplomatic ability to act a part, and his contempt for religion. All these qualities make him a complicated character calling for a complicated response of sympathy and antipathy. Our sympathy for him is probably at its height when we see him as a child and just before his death, and at its lowest ebb when we see him in relation to his victims.

Heathcliff is also at his least convincing and realistic, I think, in his role as aggressor, at least when we find him muttering as he does in Chapter XIV 'The more the worms writhe, the more I yearn to crush out their entrails', or when he threatens to ill-treat Isabella (as he does) or Edgar. These sadistic characteristics are much more repugnant than any we see in the earlier parts of the novel (foreshadowed perhaps in the little episode about the two horses in Chapter IV) and although it may not be quite accurate to say that Heathcliff deteriorates, it is, I think, true to say that it is his treatment of these three children which alienates much of our early sympathy. He remains the centre of interest and the second generation does not form a separate action.

Nevertheless, the two generations are placed together in the relationship created by strong parallelism and contrast. In this respect the novel is like the more complicated actions in Dickens or George Eliot. There is a strong resemblance in the situation: the eternal triangle which held the first generation in its tense antagonism is repeated in the second generation. Hareton and Linton are rivals, and Catherine, like her mother, first marries the wrong man. Like her mother she is tormented and hardened. But the resemblance serves mainly to bring out the differences. Linton may be superficially like the Lintons in his appearance, which charms the second Catherine as Edgar's appearance charmed her mother, but the second Catherine is not really torn between two loves. She wakes out of her adolescent response to Linton's sweetness and the proxy love-letter courtship by Heathcliff before the

marriage takes place. She is a kidnapped and reluctant
bride. Moreover, the relationship between the two
rivals is very different. They are presented com-
paratively when Catherine first meets them, but they
can really only be spoken of as rivals by implication,
since they both marry her. There is only a faint
shadow of the pull on both sides which was so strong
for the first Catherine. Unlike her mother, the second
Catherine is released by her husband's death, not her
own, and has her happy ending.

The resemblances and differences are present in
character as well as situation. Hareton is not only the
rejected one, like Heathcliff, but is of course deliberately created and distorted by Heathcliff. And the
self-created image torments its maker at the end. Heathcliff not only feels the strong affection for Hareton but
also sees him as 'a personification of my youth' whose
aspect is 'the ghost of my immortal love; of my wild
endeavours to hold my right; my degradation, my
pride, my happiness, and my anguish'. The torment
is increased by Hareton's striking physical resemblance
to Catherine. But in every important way, Hareton is
unlike Heathcliff. Instead of growing to hate the man
who degrades and deprives him, he loves him, defends
him, and laments his death. Hareton's sweetness and
gentleness is never very deeply disfigured by sullen-
ness, even when Catherine has repulsed his friendly
overtures. We may well feel, though little is said or
shown of this, that Heathcliff does indeed live in
amity with Hareton, and this reflects on both of them.
Heathcliff may superficially reproduce the deprivation
of education, the hard physical labours, and the

poverty from which he suffered, but there is never any suggestion that he can reproduce the hatred felt by Hindley Earnshaw for the young Heathcliff. Situation and character are essentially different.

The second Catherine reminds us of her mother in certain ways. Nelly points out that they shared a 'capacity for intense attachments', 'a propensity to be saucy', and 'a perverse will'. But the second Catherine is noticeably sweeter and gentler than the first, at least as she appears in Nelly's story. Nelly and Lockwood never quite give us the same Catherine, as you may see if you make the comparison. This is partly because of Nelly's partiality, and partly because of the situation in which Lockwood meets Catherine. Her gentleness, like Hareton's, can perhaps be attributed in part (without speculating too much on the effects of environment) to her upbringing. In a sense, Hareton is deprived of everything but affection. Catherine is deprived of nothing, and unlike her mother, who antagonised her father, old Earnshaw, and who was both neglected and rebuked for running wild, she is carefully nurtured and adored.

As I have already said, her relations with Hareton and Linton are very different from her mother's relations with Heathcliff and Edgar. But if we leave the basically different situation and turn to the emotions, we find some resemblances. There is no strong statement of affinity between Catherine and Hareton but it is perhaps significant that they get on very well at their first meeting. It is he who helps her to realise her ambition to climb Peniston Crag, whose 'golden rocks' she sees from the enclosed park of

Thrushcross Grange. It is he who shows her the enchantments of the Fairy Cave. Like the first Catherine and Heathcliff, though in a much slighter way, they share their adventures and their moors. Like the first Catherine and Heathcliff, they are shown eventually as forming an alliance of love and friendship in a dark and harsh house, the same house of Wuthering Heights. But between the first expedition and the final alliance there is no resemblance between the second generation and the first. And even at the end, her winning of Hareton and the combination of courtship and education is only a faint echo of the first pair and their affinities and separations. Perhaps the difference in character cannot be separated from the difference in situation. The first Catherine says that her love for Heathcliff comes out of a sharing of misery, and as the novel grows it seems apparent that this is a love which both creates and overcomes obstacles. Some of the obstacles, if not all, are of their own making. The obstacles put in the way of the second course of true love are scarcely of the lovers' own making.

There are two important passages which do seem to form a link between the two sets of lovers and the two loves. I have already quoted the first Catherine's comparison between her love for Edgar and her love for Heathcliff (pp. 33-35 above; Chapter IX in the novel). The second Catherine compares two concepts of happiness, and the comparison is made in the form of a debate with Linton:

> One time, however, we were near quarrelling.
> He said the pleasantest manner of spending a hot
> July day was lying from morning until evening on

a bank of heath in the middle of the moors, with the
bees humming dreamily about among the bloom,
and the larks singing high up overhead, and the
blue sky and bright sun shining steadily and cloud-
lessly. That was his most perfect idea of heaven's
happiness: mine was rocking in a rustling green
tree, with a west wind blowing, and bright white
clouds flitting rapidly above; and not only larks, but
throstles, and blackbirds, and linnets, and cuckoos
pouring out music on every side, and the moors
seen at a distance, broken into cool, dusky dells;
but close by great swells of long grass undulating
in waves to the breeze; and woods and sounding
water, and the whole world awake and wild with
joy. He wanted all to lie in an ecstasy of peace;
I wanted all to sparkle and dance in a glorious
jubilee. I said his heaven would be only half alive;
and he said mine would be drunk: I said I should
fall asleep in his; and he said he could not breathe
in mine, and began to grow very snappish. At last,
we agreed to try both, as soon as the right weather
came; and then we kissed each other and were
friends.   (Chapter XXIV).

Anyone making a study of *Wuthering Heights* should
compare this passage very closely with Catherine's con-
fidences to Nelly Dean (Chapter IX). For my present
purposes, a few comments will be enough. It is true
that there is some resemblance between the two sets
of distinctions being set up by both women. There is
spirit and vitality in the first Catherine's choice of
lightning and fire to express the stuff her soul and
Heathcliff's are made of, and there is spirit and vitality

D

in the second Catherine's concept of wind and motion
and birds 'pouring out music' and 'the whole world
awake and wild with joy' and the images of nature
correspond with the characters' vitality and physical
activity. There is gentleness in the image of the
moonbeam, chosen for Edgar Linton. There is cold,
perhaps in the frost, though this fits less closely, and
may only be there to express a great difference rather
than to say that Edgar is like frost. There is luxuriant
beauty in the imagery of foliage which the first Catherine uses to define her love for Edgar. There is a
gentle warm languor and beauty in Linton Heathcliff's
idea of bliss. To this extent there is similarity.

There is difference too. Lord David Cecil—and he
is not alone in this—makes much of the symbolic
implications of the setting of *Wuthering Heights*:

> The setting is a microcosm of the universal
> scheme as Emily Brontë conceived it. On the
> one hand, we have Wuthering Heights, the land
> of storm; high on the barren moorland, naked
> to the shock of the elements, the natural home of
> the Earnshaw children, fiery, untamed children of
> the storm. On the other, sheltered in the leafy
> valley below, stand Thrushcross Grange, the
> appropriate home of the children of calm, the
> gentle, passive, timid Lintons. (*Early Victorian
> Novelists*, p. 164).

I think we should notice that in Catherine's actual
comparison, there is not this distinction between the
moors and the valley. Linton's image of languid
inactivity is set on the moors (which are not always
barren) while Catherine's image of ecstasy is set in the

wooded park of the valley (which is not always sheltered). This crossing of the wires is important, and draws out attention to the possibility that Lord David Cecil's famous antithesis is—like many critical interpretations and schemes—more tidy and simple and static than the antitheses set up in the actual novel. I do not rely merely on the imagery when I make this objection: Lord David, for instance, makes his scheme work by describing Frances Earnshaw (Hindley's wife) and Isabella Linton (Heathcliff's wife) as 'children of calm'. I will not set out my reasons for disagreeing with this account of the two women but leave you to consider it for yourselves.

What I am concerned to point out is the difference between the first Catherine's lightning and fire and the second Catherine's summer wind in grass and trees. The second Catherine expresses her spirit in terms of the foliage which the first Catherine uses as a simile for the gentle and transient love she feels for Edgar. Admittedly, the two women are not talking about exactly the same thing. One is talking about love and the other about happiness. But both are also talking about their essential vitality, and both are explicitly talking about incompatibility. I want to emphasise this comparison because it draws attention not only to the flexibility of Emily Brontë's use of setting and imagery and symbol, a flexibility disregarded by Lord David Cecil, but also to the difference between the first and the second generation. Lord David does admit this difference, and explains it in terms of his antithesis between calm and storm by calling the second generation 'the offspring of both' which 'partake of both natures' which seems less wide of the mark than his account of the setting of the novel, or than his attempt to force *all* the characters into a pattern which might be used to describe *some*.

Lord David sees the end of the novel as the harmonious marriage of these opposite principles of calm and storm: 'the kindness and constancy of calm, the strength and courage of storm.' He does admit, in a footnote, that he is here doing some simplifying, since the children are not homogeneous characters: 'Hareton can be surly, Catherine wilful.' But where I most strongly disagree with his account of the novel is with its emphasis on the final establishment of harmony.

Everyone will presumably agree that there is an important difference between the havoc and disorder brought about by the love of Heathcliff and Catherine and the tranquillity and stability present in the marriage of Hareton and his Catherine. All I wish to suggest is that a question-mark hangs over the harmonious full-stop. The novel ends not only with the happy marriage but with the frustration of Heathcliff's revenge, the restoration of the property, and Nelly Dean's delight in her 'children's' happiness. As I have already said in my introduction, I do not think this novel makes a clear statement of generalisations about life. Lord David Cecil does not see the novel as morally simple, but he does apparently see it as containing a metaphysical generalisation, as setting out 'to justify the ways of God to Man', a remark which I confess I do not really understand.

Hareton and Catherine certainly have their happy marriage. They have their property restored, though it is interesting to note that the character who rejoices most in this is old Joseph, in his decidedly unsympathetic appearance at Heathcliff's deathbed: 'he fell on his knees, and raised his hands, and returned thanks that the lawful master and the ancient stock were restored to their rights'(Chapter XXXIV). It is plain that this aspect of the happy ending is not one which Emily Brontë wishes to stress. Heathcliff's frustration is also not important, since he loses interest in his revenge. Nelly seems to feel that we have moved from undesirable disorder and pain to peace and happiness, in spite of her reactions to Heathcliff's death. From the point of view of morality and commonsense, she is right.

I have already set out my belief that Nelly does not see all there is to see. The reader sees through Nelly's vision in two senses. He sees what she sees and sees the viewpoint from which she sees. And I suggest that for some readers at least there will remain the feeling that the constancy and vitality and pain in the love of Heathcliff and Catherine lies beyond the scope of her moral view. She prevents us from idealising their love blindly, and we see its defectiveness. We see its folly and selfishness and hardness largely through her eyes. Not entirely so, for both the first Catherine and Heathcliff himself insist on the true nature of Heathcliff, at least when setting out the romantic blindness of Isabella. Catherine sees him exactly as he is, which is one of the admirable qualities of her love. She tells Nelly in Chapter IX that Heathcliff's presence in her mind is not 'a pleasure, any more than I am always a pleasure to myself', and we might say that it has nothing to do with happiness. The love of Hareton and Catherine is a happy ending in the literal sense, but it seems to me that all it ends happily is their own relationship. *Wuthering Heights* is rather like a tragedy which includes a happy ending, but it is not the tragic protagonists who can end happily. It is, in my belief, the tragic protagonists, unideal and unromantic and immoral, who command an imaginative response which the happy wedded pair do not, and I see the novel as setting out harmony for some and asserting the inharmonious strength of others. Perhaps the crucial question is this: do you feel that the domestic peace of Hareton and Catherine represents a tamer and easier love than the endurance and affinity and painful rapture of Heathcliff and his Catherine?

I should like to mention here two other well-known happy endings: the reconciliations which conclude *The Tempest* and *The Winter's Tale*. Shakespeare is also combining tragic material with reconciliation, and in both plays we may be said to move from disorder to order, from the undesirable to the desirable, from error to rectitude. In both plays the harmony of the second generation triumphs over the disasters and disorders of the first. Prospero is reconciled to his enemies, his powers are properly used and properly abdicated, and we end with the marriage of Miranda and Ferdinand. There are unreconciled elements like Caliban and Antonio, and the sweetness of the lovers is that of innocence rather than experience. But there is a progression from what can be called tragedy to what can be called harmony, from the bad to the better, if not to perfection.

The Winter's Tale is a clearer and simpler example,
with no final discords. It is indeed very like *Wuthering
Heights* in its expansive treatment of two generations
and in its use of the seasonal movement from winter to
summer. The love of Perdita and Florizel reconciles
the quarrel of Sicily and Bohemia, ends the curse, and
brings the suggestions of constancy, fertility and joy
to erase the jealousy, sterility and anguish of the
first wintry part of the play. But there is, I think, no
suggestion that the love of Leontes and Hermione was
more ecstatic or more difficult than the love of these
children. In fact Shakespeare makes Perdita and Florizel move through painful obstacles also.

You may object that Emily Brontë also makes
Hareton and Catherine move through painful obstacles
to win their harmony. But I think their pain is very
much less: Hareton's degradation has not touched his
mind nor finally deprived him of love in this world.
Catherine has been freed from her marriage by Linton's
death. Moreover, to return to *The Winter's Tale*,
which follows a chronological order from which this
novel departs, the two actions are separated, whereas
Emily Brontë juxtaposes the happy lovers' harmony
with the last pains and rapture of the haunted Heathcliff. We are presented with two kinds of love, both
affirmed simultaneously. And—perhaps most important—there is nothing in the love of Perdita and
Ferdinand which we would exchange for the love of
Hermione and Leontes. The love of Heathcliff and
Catherine commands a great admiration, I suggest,
because it has not only brought disaster but has been
formed by that disaster. As Catherine says, it was

born in shared misery. And in its suffering and its vitality as well as its endurance (beyond the grave and in defiance of 'Heaven') it does at least present a serious challenge to Nelly Dean's sense of harmony. The love of Hareton and Catherine is a happy and prosperous love, but the love of Catherine and Heathcliff is the love of 'another species' and remains in tragic significance outside the order of the second generation.

Questions:

1. You may disagree with my conclusions in this section, but it will help you at least to see on what evidence they are based if you ask yourself to draw up a list of the admirable qualities in the first Catherine, and Heathcliff, and their relationship, and put it beside a similar list of the admirable qualities in the second Catherine and Hareton. If you find nothing admirable in the first generation, then you will of course be sharing Nelly Dean's view. It might then be interesting to see if you agree with me about her being at times an unreliable and inadequate guide, making mistakes and not seeing all the implications.

2. Hareton is perhaps the most completely good and attractive character in the novel. How does Hareton's relationship with Heathcliff affect our response to both characters? You should pay particular attention to what Heathcliff says about Hareton, to Hareton's behaviour to Heathcliff after he and the second Catherine have been reconciled, and to Hareton's response to Heathcliff's death.

3. What use does Emily Brontë make of setting and landscape and the seasons? Look at her descriptions, her imagery, and the reactions of the characters, not excluding Lockwood. There are some interesting details in Lockwood's description of his first and his last impressions of Wuthering Heights in Chapters XXXII and XXXIV. The last words of the novel are worth careful scrutiny.

THE TWO WORLDS

(i)

THE SUPERNATURAL WORLD

Much of the excitement and terror and tension of *Wuthering Heights* surely depends on its power of supernatural suggestion. Although there is a solid natural and domestic setting there are times when we feel that we are moving beyond the boundaries of natural events and causes. But I have used the words 'suggestion' and 'we feel' advisedly. The novel uses its machinery of ghosts and mystery in a way which we may call realistic. Emily Brontë's use of fantastic material, it might be argued, is indeed more realistic than her sister Charlotte's, even though it is Charlotte who insisted her need, as a novelist, to move away from 'elfland' into the ordinary world of sober reality. The supernatural machinery at the end of *Jane Eyre*, for instance, appears to transmit a message from Rochester to Jane in the nick of time. She leaves St. John Rivers, who is powerfully pleading with her to join him as his wife and helper, and the action of the novel is turned and concluded. In *Wuthering Heights* none of the supernatural 'activity' has this kind of influence on action. And I might add, by way of brief and relevant digression, that Emily Brontë's use of mystery and violence (so-called 'melodramatic' material) is more plausible, in my view, than Charlotte's. The ghost in *Villette* or the mad wife in *Jane Eyre* arouse fear and doubt and tension but at the expense of plausibility.

In *Wuthering Heights* the supernatural sways the response of some of the characters (not all) but does not have to be accepted as part of the action. Its reality is left tentatively in doubt, within the area of folk-superstition and dreams. As in real life, the ghosts appear in dreams or abnormal states of consciousness, or else 'appear' to other people. The two story-tellers, for instance, see ghosts only in a dream (Lockwood) or in the reflected horror and fear of other people's experience (Nelly Dean). These are ghosts which are brought into the novel subtly and tenta-tively, inviting no strenuous effort to suspend dis-belief from the sceptical reader. (The believers in ghosts may have a slightly different response to the novel but they, in their turn, do not see their ghosts transformed by last-minute materialistic explanation, as in many thrillers, including *Villette*). The question is left open.

But there are one or two genuine mysteries in the novel which should be mentioned, since they open uneasily sinister doors through which supernatural implications creep in more insistently than I may have been implying. I do not include among these mysteries the unknown origin of Heathcliff or the unknown gap in his fortune and career when he goes away and somehow gets money and an education. These mysteries cast a shadow in which Heathcliff remains, but it is not, I think, the shadow of the supernatural. The questions asked about Heathcliff by Lockwood at

the beginning of Chapter X ('Did he finish his education on the Continent, and come back a gentleman? or
did he get a sizar's place at college, or escape to
America, and earn honours by drawing blood from
his foster-country? or make a fortune more promptly
on the English highways?') or the question Nelly
Dean asks Heathcliff himself ('Have you been for a
soldier?') are questions which are never answered, but
the very nature of these questions at least suggests a
whole range of plausible explanations. We need not
fill this gap in knowledge by resorting to some
'diabolical' view of Heathcliff.

Such a view is at least entertained by Nelly when
she speculates about his origin at the end of the novel,
while Heathcliff keeps his vigil in Catherine's old room.
She tells us that Superstition asks if this origin might
have been diabolical: 'But where did he come from,
the little dark thing, harboured by a good man to his
bane?' But dawn restores her 'to common-sense'.
These gaps contribute to our sense of mystery and
uncertainty, but not because they raise unanswerable
questions.

There are, however, one or two details for which
commonsense has no answer. These are largely
connected with Lockwood's second dream in Chapter
III. He is terrified by the 'ghost' of 'Catherine Linton'.
She picks up his idle words 'not if you beg for twenty
years' and wails 'It is twenty years . . . twenty years.
I've been a waif for twenty years'.

Lockwood draws our attention to the strange
coincidence that the name in the dream is indeed the
right name: 'Why did I think of *Linton*? I had read

Earnshaw twenty times for Linton'. The other materials in the dream are attributable to the information he has gleaned from Catherine's jottings just before he falls asleep, but the name of Linton does have the effect of making the ghost appear to have a 'status' outside Lockwood's own dreaming, and at this stage we are invited to see at least the possibility of the dream as haunting rather than dream. We might add to this, though less certainly, the detail of the time, the 'twenty years'. Our attention is not directed towards this detail, as it is towards the name, and 'twenty years' may indeed be no more than a good round number, since Lockwood notes that Catherine's Testament bears a date 'some quarter of a century back'. But if we do take the trouble to check the time since Catherine's death, which the ghost might be thought to allude to, we will find that seventeen years have passed: the first Catherine dies when her daughter is born, and Lockwood's comment that the second Catherine does not look seventeen is confirmed when Nelly tells us that Catherine is eighteen when she marries Hareton in 1802. But it is roughly twenty years since Catherine lost Heathcliff. She married Edgar Linton three years after his father died, we are told, and he dies, with his wife, on catching Catherine's fever which starts with her exposure and distress on the night Heathcliff leaves *Wuthering Heights*. Allowing some time for her pregnancy, we discover that it is probably between twenty and twenty-one years since Catherine was bereaved, not of life, but of Heathcliff. Since the crying ghost is a child rather than an adult it may be that Emily Brontë is suggesting that it is the fifteen-year-old Catherine who haunts her old room at the Heights, lamenting the loss of her love. This is another detail which Lockwood does not know at the time of his dream, and though it is not apparent without doing some research, it does perhaps fit with the conspicuous coincidence of the name. Together these are perhaps the only really strong suggestions of real ghosts. It is significant that they are there to be seized on or passed over, not disturbing the tentative presentation of supernatural activity.

They do however draw our attention to other smaller coincidences pointing in the same direction. Lockwood dreams that Catherine is trying to get back to her old room, and this forms a link with an earlier dream (which the reader and Lockwood are told about later) when Catherine imagines in her delirium that she is back in her old room. In Chapter XII her mind wanders and she thinks she can see her own face reflected in the 'black press' and she insists that the room is haunted. She also tells Nelly that when she first collapses, after she locks herself in her room, that she lies on the floor thinking 'that I was enclosed in the oak-panelled bed at home'. It is also clear from Heathcliff's narrative in Chapter XXIX that he feels her haunting presence in her old room: 'she was either outside the window, or sliding back the panels, or entering the room, or even resting her darling head on the same pillow'. And at the end we have the last coincidence, for Heathcliff has died before the open window, his hand grazed as Catherine's ghostly hand is grazed in Lockwood's dream.

When Lockwood's dream makes him declare that

the room is haunted, in other words, there is some backing for this elsewhere in the book. But it is Heathcliff rather than the room who is being haunted: Catherine returns to her old home denying the life she has spent with Edgar at Thrushcross Grange. And it is here that *place* is significant in a wider sense: she tells Nelly her dream of exile in Heaven in Chapter IX. This is apparently not the dream which she begins but is forbidden to tell by the superstitious Nelly. But it answers to her description of 'dreams that have stayed with me ever after, and changed my ideas . . . gone through and through me, like wine through water, and altered the colour of my mind'. In this dream, also one of being cut off from Heathcliff, she longs to return, and does return, not to the house but to the moors outside. Her longing for the air and freedom of the moors is related to another strand in the suggestions of haunting—the ghosts wandering together on the moors who are seen by 'the country folk' including old Joseph and the little boy. Catherine feels imprisoned in the Grange and she also feels cut off from air: her window has to be opened in her sick delirium just as it is opened to let in the rain on Heathcliff's corpse. Catherine, in life, and, by suggestion, in death, struggles against bars and barriers. Wherever she is she seems to be struggling against the barriers which keep her from Heathcliff.

There is, however, one place when she seems to be struggling against more than this barrier. In Chapter XV she says that she 'will not be at peace' and tells him that if he is ever distressed by a word of hers after her death he can think that she feels the same

underground. In Chapter XII she dares him to come
with her back home past 'Gimmerton Kirk' and says
that she'll 'not lie there alone and will not rest until
he is with her'. Later in Chapter XV she seems to be
thinking not so much of Heathcliff as of life and death,
seeing life, in this world or her sick body, as a 'shattered prison' and 'wearying to escape into that glorious
world, and to be always there: not seeing it dimly
through tears'.

This last passage may seem inconsistent with her
earlier dream of desolation in Heaven and even with
her insistence that she will not rest in her grave without
Heathcliff. It may merely represent her distaste for
present existence, implying her exile from Heathcliff.
It may imply that only beyond the grave can her
vitality find freedom. It seems to me to be very
uncertain that Catherine can be said to long for conventional religious bliss, though this is how Nelly Dean
interprets the longing in Chapter XVI. We cannot
separate the supernatural suggestions from the religious
issues raised in the novel, and one of the difficulties, I
suggest, lies in the apparent contradiction between the
Christian supernatural and the supernatural implications of Catherine and Heathcliff, in vision and in
longings as well as in their suggested hauntings.

Let us set out some of the things Catherine and
Heathcliff say about death. Catherine dreams of being
miserable in Heaven, she tells Heathcliff she will not
rest in her grave, she longs to escape from this life
into a 'glorious world'. Heathcliff says that he will be
alive while his soul is in the grave, stills his torment
by uncovering her face in that grave, and makes

arrangements to be buried beside her and have the sides of their coffins broken so that their dust will mingle. And there is no doubt that Heathcliff believes that her ghost haunts him and that he will join her. Lord David Cecil is helpful when he speaks of 'Immortality of Spirit in this world' though I cannot agree with him when he quotes Nelly Dean as being in agreement with such a view. Nelly says that when she looks on Catherine's corpse, her doubts about her eternal deserts are stilled and she feels that 'her spirit is at home with God'. But this is not how Catherine speaks of her survival after death. Even giving weight to her sick longing to escape the body's prison, she seems to be consistent in longing for freedom and vitality, though in no clearly discernible orthodox sense, and her actions (suggested rather than stated) after death seem to imply that this freedom and vitality must be shared by Heathcliff: what her death releases her into is imagined as limited by not having 'him with her'. This insistence on a love which needs to leave the body, though decidedly rare and strange, is perhaps one of those elements in the novel which makes us feel that Hareton and the second Catherine have an easier *and* more restricted existence than Heathcliff and the first Catherine.

The novel does little more than suggest these things. We find various attitudes expressed and suggested about life and death, and life beyond death. The novel falls into no recogniseable doctrinal pattern. Even Nelly Dean, whose sensibilities and speculations are differentiated both from Joseph's brand of religion and from Lockwood's, is not on absolutely sure ground.

E

The emphasis is thrown less on the problem of Heaven and Hell than on to the theme of deprivation and union. Catherine is released from her deprivation and conflict. Heathcliff is tormented by feeling her near but out of reach and he too is at last released from this deprivation and torment. We do not need to know what Emily Brontë thinks actually happens to Catherine or Heathcliff in supernatural terms to see what the supernatural suggestion makes very plain—the extent of their vitality and affinity and separation in love. Heathcliff's last pangs of fear and pain and rapture are made exquisitely clear by the sense we have of the haunting presence, but what is important is that we should see him seeing the ghost.

For readers who feel confused by these varying attitudes towards life and death it may be helpful to explain that all these attitudes can be found in Emily Brontë's poetry, sometimes in love poems, sometimes in religious poems, and most often in love poems expressing emotion in terms of concepts of death and life after death. What we have, I think, is less a consistent theological pattern than a dramatisation of different points of view. I have not the space to discuss the poems in detail but will merely give brief references, all to C. W. Hatfield's edition of *The Complete Poems of Emily Jane Brontë*.

Hatfield points to two poems which 'identify the mind of the writer with the author of that powerful story *Wuthering Heights*'. One is a poem expressing something of Catherine's desire to leave the 'shattered prison' and find liberty (No. 146) and another is a poem expressing Catherine's preference for familiar

Earth over Heaven: 'We would not leave our native
home. For *any* world beyond the Tomb' (No. 149).
To these I should like to add her last poem, 'No
coward soul' (No. 191) which shows the kind of faith
in God *not* expressed by Catherine but rising above the
various 'creeds' demonstrated by, say, old Joseph or
implied in Lockwood and Nelly. There is a poem
belonging to the Gondal series (spoken by an invented
character) which comes very near to expressing Heathcliff's sense of leaving life in the grave: 'All my life's
bliss is in the grave with thee' and his sense of pain and
rapture, though here it is combined with the sense that
life can continue 'without the aid of joy' and that the
speaker, a woman, must not 'Indulge in Memory's
rapturous pain':

'Once drinking deep of that divinest anguish,
How could I seek the empty world again?' (No. 182).

There is the sense of death as release in another
Gondal poem, containing the ecstatic lines which were
familiar to many readers before it was discovered that
they were part of a long poem spoken about Hope, as
Herald of Death, by another invented character:

'Then dawns the Invisible, the Unseen its truth
reveals;
My outward sense is gone, my inward essence feels—
Its wings are almost free, its home, its harbour found;
Measuring the gulf it stoops and dares the final
bound!

Oh, dreadful is the check—intense the agony
When the ear begins to hear and the eye begins to
see;

When the pulse begins to throb, the brain to think
  again,
The soul to feel the flesh and the flesh to feel the
  chain!'   (No. 190)

There is the sense of death as peace and repose, as in
Nelly's reaction to the deaths of Catherine and Lockwood's reactions to the graves of all three, in more
than one poem, but very strikingly in No. 181, which
ends:

'O let me die, that power and will
Their cruel strife may close,
And vanquished Good, victorious Ill
Be lost in one repose.'

and also contains the lines

'No promised Heaven, these wild Desires
Could all or half fulfil;
No threatened Hell, with quenchless fires,
Subdue this quenchless will!'

Some of these show interesting parallels with
attitudes expressed within the novel, but their chief
importance, as I see it, is that they show a variety of
dramatised views of life and death. The Gondal poems
also reveal other parallel situations of deprivation,
anguish, jealousy, and revenge, but one of their most
significant revelations is this variation in attitudes to
life and death, usually in love-poems. *Wuthering
Heights* is a novel which raises, without definitely
answering, questions about survival and religion,
questions both ethical and metaphysical, but what we
can be definite about is their emotional impact. It is

a story which uses but does not rely on religious and superstitious possibilities of survival, and these possibilities are not expressed directly by the author but dramatically, by different characters at different times. This variation is one of the difficulties of the novel, but these difficulties can at least be bypassed if we see that the author is not setting out a firmly Christian scheme, like Charlotte in *Jane Eyre*, but is using both the conventional and the unconventional attitudes to religion, the subjective and the superstitious appearances of the supernatural, in order to create a tragic definition of love.

Questions.

1. Write an essay on *Wuthering Heights* as a 'ghost-story'.

2. Emily Brontë excels in the presentation of abnormal states of mind. Try to analyse either her portrayal of Catherine's delirium after the quarrel with Edgar or Heathcliff's final state before his death, bringing out the importance of these episodes to the novel as a whole.

3. What difference might it have made if Lockwood had been made to 'see' Catherine's ghost in a waking state instead of in a dream? What difference might it have made if Nelly had been made to 'see' the ghost of Catherine at the end?

4. Try to collect as many attitudes to death and the after-life as you can find, and say how they are expressive of individual characters and how they fit together in the novel as a whole.

5. Nelly Dean is carefully contrasted with old

Joseph in religious attitude. Find some specific instances of this contrast and say what effects they have. What are we told about the religious upbringing of Catherine, Heathcliff, and Hareton, and is this relevant to the later course of events?

6. I might have mentioned one more gap in the information given us by the novelist: we are never told whether the sexton carried out Heathcliff's instructions about the coffins. How do you explain this omission?

7. The dreams in *Wuthering Heights* have various functions. Do you think they are also realistic attempts at conveying the nature of dreams?

8. I said in my Introduction (page i) that the external 'adventures' were expressive of internal adventures. Is this true of the supernatural suggestions in the novel?

THE NATURAL WORLD

On the last two pages of the novel we have some of the strongest supernatural suggestion. Nelly Dean tells of the funeral of Heathcliff, with no religious rites, according to his wish, though she says nothing of his directions about the coffins. She says 'I hope its tenant sleeps as soundly' which modifies old Joseph's comment 'Th'divil's harried off his soul' but immediately tells of the country folk who swear that he walks, and of her encounter with the little boy who has seen 'Heathcliff and a woman, yonder, under t'nab'. She sees nothing but 'neither the sheep nor he would go on'. She adds, 'He probably raised the phantoms from thinking, as he traversed the moors alone, on the nonsense he has heard his parents and companions repeat' but qualifies this by saying, 'Yet, still, I don't like being out in the dark now'. And when Lockwood says lightly that Wuthering Heights will soon be shut up 'For the use of such ghosts as choose to inhabit it' she rebukes him: 'No, Mr. Lockwood . . . I believe the dead are at peace; but it is not right to speak of them with levity'. In Chapter XVI she has asked him, 'Do you believe such people *are* happy in the other world, sir?' and he has refused to answer.

But Lockwood is left with the last word, a word slightly different from Nelly's questioning comment on Catherine's eternal rest and her tremulous hopes for Heathcliff's repose. He sees the three graves in the peace of the summer night and their appearance suggests nothing but repose:

> I sought, and soon discovered, the three headstones on the slope next the moor: the middle one grey, and half buried in heath: Edgar Linton's only harmonised by the turf and moss creeping up its foot: Heathcliff's still bare.
>
> I lingered round them, under that benign sky; watched the moths fluttering round the heath and harebells, listened to the soft wind breathing through the grass, and wondered how anyone could ever imagine unquiet slumbers for the sleepers in that quiet earth. (Chapter XXXIV).

As I have already suggested when discussing Lockwood's character and function, this last word is not necessarily the perfect summary of our whole reaction to the end. This is not a fantasy where supernatural or mysterious events and causes move freely in and out of the action, distorting the appearances of the solid material world and the solid rational explanations. From the beginning we have seen the irrational passions and the supernatural suggestions controlled in this way by being placed in the context of 'normal' commonsense and familiar objects and routine. Even if we learn, as I believe we should, not to rely too securely on the rational explanations of Lockwood and the rational though slightly more superstitious responses of Nelly Dean, there is no doubt that what we may call the realism of the novel owes much to their presence. They are ordinary and familiar. They form a plausible bridge between the reader and the story of 'another species' which lies at the novel's heart. And I want to end, in this last section, by trying to give some account of the solid roots of the strange actions and wild passions. This will entail some repetition, since it is a subject I have already touched on in the first section.

In Chapter Fourteen of the *Biographia Literaria*, Coleridge explains how he and Wordsworth planned the *Lyrical Ballads*, and his brief comment on his own contribution, poetry in which 'the incidents and agents were to be, in part at least, supernatural' has some relevance to a study of *Wuthering Heights*. 'The excellence aimed at' he says, was to consist in the interesting of the affections by the dramatic truth of such emotions, as would naturally accompany such situations, supposing them real'.

Both aim and excellence are best illustrated by *The Ancient Mariner*. In this poem the incidents and agents are certainly more plainly supernatural than those in *Wuthering Heights* but the combination of realism and fantasy is by no means dissimilar. *Wuthering Heights* has the realism of its emotional vividness, not merely as shown in the 'dramatic truth' of Catherine and Heathcliff's wild passions and strange history, but also as shown in the dramatic truth of the other characters. The strange history is framed in the ordinary world inhabited by Hareton and Catherine, victims of the strangeness and wildness but eventually emerging to lead their ordinary lives. It is framed too, as we have seen, in the point of view of Lockwood and Nelly Dean.

At the end we see Hareton and the second Catherine walking unafraid on the moors, just as Lockwood is

unafraid even though he is visiting the churchyard at
night—he who began by dreaming of ghosts. The
familiar ordinary impression made, even if not con-
clusively, at the end of the novel, owes much not only
to the impression these characters have made throughout the novel, but also to the natural setting and its
solidity. It is in stormy winter that people are afraid
in *Wuthering Heights* and the peaceful appearances at the
end are the appearances of summer. Lockwood
prefers the moors in summer, of course, and the last
reassuring words rely significantly on hints of the
season's limitations. The 'autumn storms' are yet to
come, the heath and harebells are a part of the transient
foliage, the wind will not always be soft, and the moths
will stop their fluttering. But if the whole novel is still
vibrating in our mind, we will be aware of the double
implications of such a landscape. After all, we began in
storm. After all, we do not know whether or not Heathcliff's dust is mingling with Catherine's beneath the
quiet earth in final assertion of their defiance of death
and religious rites. The 'any one' who *is* in a position
to 'imagine unquiet slumbers for the sleepers in that
quiet earth' might well be the reader of the novel. But
the point I want to stress here is that the reader is
throughout presented not only with the wild history
but with the soberness of ordinary people and real
nature. A novel which concentrated more purely on
the passions and mysteries of Heathcliff and his
Catherine would be more romantically remote from
ordinary life. It would leave out the range of human
experience which includes the spectators, like Lockwood and Nelly, or the peaceful and fortunate, like

Hareton and Catherine. It would leave out the views of such ordinary people which form the medium for the strange history, a medium which both holds it at a distance and allows us to make up our own minds about its meaning and values. But it would also leave out a great deal within that strange history itself.

The haunted Ancient Mariner's exotic landscape might be more remote and yet less exotic were it not for the constant reference to English woods and birds and peaceful familiar nature. His dreadful experiences might be less moving if we did not hear them narrated against the ordinary festive life of the marriage, the rose-red bride, and the reluctant Wedding-Guest who has to stay outside the church and listen. They would certainly be less terrible and less recognisable if we did not see his terror through the fascinated gaze of this ordinary and detached spectator. When we come to the shooting of the albatross, for instance, there is a pause while the story breaks off and we have the Wedding-Guest reacting in horror to the expression on the story-teller's face and his inability to go straight on with the story.

All these things are true of the less explicitly and mechanically supernatural suggestions and strange passions of our novel. Charlotte Brontë, in her second Preface to *Wuthering Heights*, tells us that without Heathcliff's feeling for Hareton and Nelly we would not see him as a human being, but 'say he was child neither of Lascar nor gipsy, but a man's shape animated by demon life—a Ghoul—an Afreet'. It is a pity that Charlotte does not say something about Catherine as well as Heathcliff, and her comment that his love for

Catherine 'is a sentiment fierce and inhuman' is one
you should think hard about, since it seems at least
open to argument. But it is generally true, I think,
that Heathcliff and Catherine are made real by their
relationships with other characters and with their
environment.

Think of that early Christmas party, where Nelly
watches Catherine's conflict between her delight in her
grand new friends and her love for the disgraced
Heathcliff, as she puts up some show of eating her
dinner. Think of the earlier scene where Heathcliff
and Catherine gaze through the window of Thrushcross
Grange at the 'splendid place carpeted with crimson'
and the Linton children quarrelling over their dog.
Or the scene where Catherine returns from her stay at
the Grange, in elegant ringlets and the new dress
which is both a slightly self-conscious pleasure and a
barrier between her and the dogs, the dirty Heathcliff,
and even Nelly Dean, 'all flour making the Christmas
cake'. All these scenes are socially and visually real
and solid. We see the upholstery, the drops and chains
of the chandelier, the enchanted vision for the two
wild children from the Heights. The characters
inhabit the real world of places, things, and activity.
Nelly Dean does her dusting while Edgar Linton gets
his first taste of Catherine's temper. Heathcliff decides
to be a good boy and asks Nelly to make him clean and
tidy. And this solid environment continues throughout
the novel. Isabella makes lumpy porridge on her first
inauspicious return from her elopement with Heathcliff. Nelly worries because Heathcliff is not eating his
meals, and it is real food which he accepts and then is

forced to neglect. I have already said something about the way in which the characters are shown in relationship with Nelly's solid ordinariness, and an important aspect of this kind of realism is the solid portrayal of environment too.

Natural details, as well as social and domestic ones, play their part. Consider the moving moment when Nelly goes out, after Catherine's death, to find Heathcliff standing under the ash-tree: 'He had been standing a long time in that position, for I saw a pair of ousels passing and repassing scarcely three feet from him, busy in building their nest, and regarding his proximity no more than a piece of timber' (Chapter XVI). Heathcliff's 'knowledge' of the death is tethered to this ordinary detail. It is given substance and made more moving by the detail and its implications.

Consider the wild and hysterical scene when Catherine pulls her pillow to pieces and arranges the feathers on the sheet:

'That's a turkey's' she murmured to herself; 'and this is a wild duck's; and this is a pigeon's. Ah, they put pigeon's feathers in the pillows—no wonder I couldn't die! Let me take care to throw it on the floor when I lie down. And here is a moor-cock's; and this—I should know it among a thousand—it's a lapwing's. Bonny bird; wheeling over our heads in the middle of the moor. It wanted to get to its nest, for the clouds had touched the swells, and it felt rain coming. This feather was picked up from the heath, the bird was not shot: we saw its nest in the winter, full of little skeletons. Heathcliff set a trap over it, and the old ones dare not come. I made him promise he'd never shoot a lapwing after that, and he didn't. Yes, here are more! Did he shoot my lapwings, Nelly? Are they red, any of them! Let me look.' (Chapter XII).

In many ways this is a wild strange speech, rather like Ophelia's flower speech in *Hamlet* in being both fey and precise. Nelly is frightened and answers, as commonsense usually does, by telling Catherine to pull herself together: 'Give over with that baby-work!' But the speech is a fine example of Emily Brontë's realism as well as of her ability to delineate abnormal states of consciousness. The trap and the little skeletons have a sinister reference to the future as well as the past, but they are more than a symbol. They are a part of actual things and experiences and places: the disturbed mind lovingly identifies the real feathers, and the recognition brings with it real memories. When we think of Heathcliff as a diabolical figure, or even as a man whose love for Catherine is 'fierce and inhuman' we forget such details as this, which create the world of childish joys and compansionship in which this love grew up. When a little later, Catherine tells Nelly of her hallucination of grief and misery in which the last seven years 'grew a blank' and she returned to the misery of her separation from Heathcliff we have a bare and violent strained expression of emotion. It is the small solid details, natural or domestic, like the feathers or the flour on Nelly's hands, that make the love seem human and recogniseable at least in origin. Nelly's response, like the response of the Wedding-Guest, but much more intimate and involved, gives us the sense of ordinary relationships so that Catherine and Heathcliff are not seen entirely in isolation, as belonging to 'another species', but it is the scenes and objects, as well as the people, which contribute to the feeling that the strange passions and events take place in a familiar landscape.

So that when we come to the last description of the three graves we have already become solidly habituated to the rhythm of the seasons, both in actual description and in the imagery used by the characters. The natural setting, as I have suggested earlier, is not a mere set of symbols. It has foliage which changes, creatures which move, weather which shifts. At few points in the novel—not even in the wildest accounts of delirium and passion and anguish—can we say that there is no link with the ordinary world. We have to except the dreams, and these are frankly present as dreams. The few sinister crannies I mentioned, through which suggestion leaks which cannot be always rationally answered, are the more frightening and moving because they are cracks in a recognisable and solid world. If *Wuthering Heights* is one of the strangest and most poetic of novels, it is not an unrealistic story.

Questions

1. Give an account of any one scene in the novel which you would call realistic.

2. Think of some of the ways in which the child-hood scenes between Heathcliff and Catherine explain and make more human their adult passions.

3. Do you get the impression that the characters in the novel have a daily round and routine to attend

to, or that they are shown, like speakers in lyric poetry, as disembodied expressions of emotion?

4.   Choose some examples of language which you would describe as realistic, and some examples of language you would describe differently.

5.   Pick some examples of natural description and say how far they exist for emotional expression and how far they give you the impression of a 'familiar landscape'.

6.   Examine the 'realism' of such minor characters as Joseph, Kenneth, and Zillah.

SECTION FOUR

AN ANALYSIS OF CHAPTER XVII

It was not until I had decided to take this interesting transitional chapter for detailed commentary that I discovered that it does in fact come halfway through the novel, providing us with an example of the careful construction of *Wuthering Heights*. It begins with Isabella's departure from Heathcliff and the Heights, and the story which she tells is one of her two important contributions to the narrative, as a story-teller. It moves on to a short compressed middle section, which covers the passage of six months, in which Linton Heathcliff is born, the second Catherine, as a baby, begins to 'melt' her father's 'coldness', and Hindley Earnshaw dies. At the end of the chapter we move back into dramatic close-up, with the death and funeral of Hindley, which leaves Heathcliff in legal possession of Wuthering Heights. In terms of actual plot, therefore, it is a crucial chapter, containing the decisive events of Isabella's flight, Linton's birth, Edgar's attachment to his child, his failure to take Hareton from Heathcliff, and the first major victory of Heathcliff, itself made especially decisive after we have seen Hindley's attempt on his life. It also begins the story of the second generation, not only in the actual record of births, but in the details of Linton's ailing peevishness, Edgar's affection for Catherine, and Heathcliff's stated intention to rear Hareton as a crooked tree.

The very beginning of the chapter is a moment of

F

transition. The previous chapter ends with the funeral
of Catherine, and this one begins on the next day, a
Saturday. The first thing to notice is what Ruskin
called 'the pathetic fallacy', a rather misleading term
which is frequently used and less frequently under-
stood. It is perhaps better replaced by another term,
'sympathetic weather or landscape'. Ruskin used
'pathetic fallacy' to refer to the poetic identification of
human action and feeling with appropriate natural
imagery. If the poet wants to show joy, he may
heighten his emotional expression with a description
of sunshine and flowers. If he wants to show melancholy, he may use a bleak landscape or rain. If he
wants to show torment or fury, he may use wind and
storm. 'Sympathetic weather' is more than a matter of
imagery in this novel. The actual landscape, as everyone
recognises, is itself very significant, though, as I have
tried to show, by no means simple. In this chapter we
begin with a change from summer weather to winter:

That Friday made the last of our fine days for
a month. In the evening, the weather broke; the
wind shifted from south to north-east, and brought
rain first, and then sleet and snow. On the
morrow one could hardly imagine that there had
been three weeks of summer: the primroses and
crocuses were hidden under wintry drifts; the larks
were silent, the young leaves of the early trees
smitten and blackened. And dreary, and chill, and
dismal, that morrow did creep over! My master
kept his room; I took possession of the lonely
parlour, converting it into a nursery: and there I
was, sitting with the moaning doll of a child laid

on my knee; rocking it to and fro, and watching, meanwhile, the still driving flakes build up the uncurtained window, when the door opened, and some person entered, out of breath and laughing! Catherine's coffin was strewn with 'flowers and scented leaves': she is dead, and summer is over. This is not literally true: the Northern spring's uncertainty allows the novelist to ring these changes, and make the unexpected and untimely weather into a kind of elegy for Catherine. She is silent, like the birds she has loved; smitten young, like the spring leaves; buried under the snow, like the crocuses her husband gathered for her. But because the novelist uses these associations indirectly, and does not say as I have done 'She is like the birds and leaves and flowers', the effect of this turn in the weather is not confined to such an elegeic reminder. The actual dismal day also reflects the loneliness and grief of the house after the funeral: the desolation of Nelly and Edgar are given moving emphasis in the natural scene. These are associations which we all share: this is a vivid and economical way of lamenting Catherine's death and showing the house of mourning, where even the newborn child can arouse no joy, only adding its wailing to the grief. Then the loneliness and dismalness of the grief within and the winter weather outside is suddenly broken by Isabella's hysterical laughter. The scene is most carefully set, establishing the present, reminding us of the past, and creating a dramatic contrast with the entry of Isabella. It also makes a fit beginning for the whole chapter, which, as I have said, begins a new stage in suffering for all these people.

If we are analysing a chapter in this close fashion, we may either work slowly through, following the sequence, or take one strand and trace its appearance and function. Initially, we should probably try to take in as much as possible, in the fullness of the actual text, but I want here to jump ahead and say a little more about the sympathetic weather in the rest of the chapter.

Isabella's entry actually keeps the weather before us, though in its violence rather than its melancholy. She has come to the Grange from the Heights, defying the weather as Catherine and Heathcliff have done and are to do on several occasions. More like a child of storm than a child of calm, she comes in dripping with snow and water, scratched, bruised, and exhausted, but laughing in spite of her 'predicament' and ignoring Nelly's distress and practical suggestions. Little is said about this, but both here and at the end of her story, when she says that she 'bounded, leaped, and flew down the steep road; then quitting its windings, shot direct across the moor, rolling over banks, and wading through marshes' there is the implication that the violent weather is nothing to the violence from which she is running away. 'When the mind's free, the body's delicate' says Lear, and Isabella's indifference to the snow has something of this suggestion, especially when we remember that she is pregnant—Nelly refers delicately to this when she says 'and in your condition!'

The body's indifference to nature has already emphasised the mind's anguish in the previous scene where Heathcliff has stood under the ash tree all night, soaked with the dew. It is to be emphasised again when Heathcliff digs at the earth over Catherine's grave in the north wind, or when his dead face and throat are finally found 'washed with rain'. Isabella is wide of the mark when she taunts Heathcliff for not being able to 'bear a shower of snow', saying that 'the moment a blast of winter returns, you must run for shelter!' as he stands at the window, calling 'let me in' as Catherine does in Lockwood's dream. In this scene, where Hindley and Isabella lock Heathcliff out, his desperation and isolation are given emphasis by the weather. Isabella sees him standing outside: 'hair and clothes were whitened with snow, and his sharp cannibal teeth, revealed by cold and wrath, gleamed through the dark'. Two pages earlier, Isabella has said 'It seemed so dismal to go upstairs, with the wild snow blowing outside, and my thoughts continually reverting to the kirkyard and the new-made grave!' Both violence and the dismal thoughts of the dead are mirrored in the wild weather. 'A sad tale's best for winter' says Mamillius in *The Winter's Tale*, and winter has seemed best for many a sad tale. It is not for nothing that this one begins in winter, and the weather is never unimportant in *Wuthering Heights*, as I have suggested more briefly in my last chapter. It is on rainy nights, Joseph says, that he has seen the ghosts of Catherine and Heathcliff. It is 'a dark evening, threatening thunder' when Nelly meets the little boy crying with fear because he thinks he can see 'Heathcliff and a woman'—a marvellous touch, by the way, for he is too young to have known Catherine and so would say just 'a woman'.

We have already seen how both Catherine and Nelly describe other characters in imagery drawn from the natural world. In this chapter there are just one or two examples of metaphors related to the significant weather: Heathcliff's eyes 'rained down tears'; Edgar's coldness 'melted as fast as snow in April'; Heathcliff says to Hareton, 'we'll see if one tree won't grow as crooked as another, with the same wind to twist it!' *Wuthering Heights* provides us with many examples of the pointlessness of looking only at the imagery of a novel, without relating similes and metaphors to the actual scene and action.

If we were making a study of the linguistic details of this chapter, it would not be these few natural images which would first strike our attention. We should probably first notice the religious associations which are constantly raised, and particularly the use of diabolical suggestion in the descriptions of Heathcliff. The strongest case for Heathcliff's diabolical nature is made by Isabella. She calls him 'my accursed', 'incarnate goblin', 'monster', and speaks of his 'devilish nature', 'his kin beneath' and 'his own black father', while Hindley contributes 'fiend' and 'hellish villain'. In one of the most extraordinary images in the novel, Isabella describes Heathcliff's eyes as 'the clouded windows of hell', adding, 'the fiend which usually looked out, however, was dimmed and drowned'.

These words remind us of that later passage when even Nelly is tempted to think of him as 'a ghoul or a vampire' and the 'sharp cannibal teeth', as Isabella

describes them, come into full view at the end when
Nelly describes the dead face with the sneering 'sharp
white teeth'. But in this scene Nelly is in full possession
of her common-sense and humanity and rebukes Isabella
for praying that the 'monster' should 'be blotted out of
creation':

> 'Hush, hush! He's a human being . . . . Be
> more charitable; there are worse men than he is
> yet'!

At this point we must stop looking at the words the
characters use and look at their individual bias and
also at their actions and attitudes. Isabella's violent
story takes up a large part of the chapter, and it is worth
looking closely at the impression it makes as a whole.
She has already made one contribution as a storyteller, in the letter she writes to Nelly (Chapter XIII)
and it is technically necessary that she should give her
eye-witness account of scenes where Nelly and Lockwood have to be absent. This account of hers is plainly
much more than the mere filling in of such a gap in the
story. Her point of view, like Lockwood's and Nelly's,
has its special bias. It is perhaps in his relationship
with Isabella, from the first exploitation of her love to
the last exploitation of their child, that Heathcliff is
at his worst. This chapter adds to our impression of
his physical cruelty, and the strong language of her
hatred is clearly justified. But it is justified from her
point of view: it is not the total impression we have of
Heathcliff. Like Lockwood and Nelly, she presents an
extreme and personal judgement which prevents the
reader from making a similarly extreme judgement.
Nelly's contradiction is only one of the moments in

this chapter where we are reminded of the personal nature of Isabella's attack. Isabella is a sympathetic character: her feeling for Heathcliff, Catherine's insensitive response to it, her ignorance, and her sufferings, all combine to awaken sympathy for her endurance and her spirit. In this scene she has a certain harsh humour and sound commonsense: she judges very neatly just what she may and may not do. And her feeling for Catherine comes out very finely, both when she sees the child and when she speaks of Catherine's illness and death. She is by no means adequately judged by Heathcliff's contempt, though that too is explicable by the character and the circumstances.

Her great attack on Heathcliff is dramatically prefaced by her laughter, her disregard for her physical state, and her smashing and burning of the wedding-ring. Her story of deliberately extinguished love and of physical violence, builds up our revulsion for Heathcliff. But in two very important ways—apart from the little contradiction from Nelly—the Heathcliff we see through Isabella's eyes is more human than monstrous.

First, there is the vivid record of Heathcliff's grief, which comes to us now in Isabella's language of hate, in its way a more impressive medium than Nelly's narrative in the previous chapter. There is nothing extraordinary in his lamentation before the dying Catherine, or his revelations to Nelly. But when we see him weeping passionately in the company of the upbraiding Joseph, the murderous Hindley, and the spiteful Isabella, there is the impression of passionate obsession and isolation.

Moreover, even Isabella's sense that he is a fiend exacerbates and enlarges our impression of his grief and love. She sees his eyes as the 'windows of hell' but even she cannot fail to see that the 'fiend' is 'drowned and dimmed'. It is one of the most violent scenes in the novel, both in language and in action. He is attacked and threatened by Hindley, goaded by Isabella, but there is no release from his tormenting love. The record of suffering is impressive because it is made by an antagonistic witness. It is also impressive because of the struggle and malevolence shown by everyone, not by Heathcliff alone.

What is most repulsive in Heathcliff is his steady commitment to revenge, and this gets strong emphasis in this scene, where we see him with three of the chief victims, Isabella, Hindley, and Hareton. It is worth noticing that Emily Brontë shows not only his inhumanity but theirs: he is not the only one driven to revenge. Isabella attacks his cruelty and loss of feeling, but describes herself in terms which bracket her with Heathcliff. 'People feel with their hearts' she says, 'and since he has destroyed mine, I have not power to feel for him'. When Hindley tries to get her to help kill Heathcliff she recoils not for moral reasons but from her sense of expediency: 'I'd be glad of a retaliation that wouldn't recoil on myself.' She tells Nelly that in her secret heart she thought that it would be 'a blessing' for her if Hindley should 'send Heathcliff to his right abode', and insists that 'conscience never reproached me'. When Heathcliff manages to disarm Hindley she is disappointed. Her violent heartless feeling comes out not only in these feelings of revenge, but also in her goading of Heathcliff. She goes on flicking him on the raw, blaming him for Catherine's death, telling him that Catherine and Edgar were happy before he came back, and—the most important point of all—echoing Catherine's talk about degradation.

Heathcliff throws the knife at her, and if we not do remember the exact point at which he does this, we have failed to recognise Emily Brontë's subtle manipulation of sympathy and antipathy. He throws the knife just after she says this:

> ... if poor Catherine had trusted you, and assumed the ridiculous, contemptible, degrading title of Mrs. Heathcliff, she would soon have presented a similar picture! *She* wouldn't have borne your abominable behaviour quietly: her detestation and disgust must have found voice.

Heathcliff had first left Wuthering Heights (Chapter IX) when he heard Catherine say, 'It would degrade me to marry Heathcliff now'. What is important here is not so much, I think, that this make us understand why he threw the knife at Isabella, but that we are taken back, in a kind of re-enactment, to the earlier turning point in the action. It is especially important that this should take place in a scene where Hindley's wrongs are so strongly emphasised, and where Heathcliff's intentions of degrading Hareton are made so explicit.

Hindley is here presented as a fairly sympathetic revenger, and his insistence that 'treachery and violence are a just return' again show that Heathcliff is not singled out in his revengeful feelings, and show too that the action is not one which springs from the inhuman nature of Heathcliff but has the form of a feud, with the vicious circle of injustice and wild justice, wrongs and revenge.

To sum up then, this is a scene which shows how we must swing from antipathy to sympathy: if we see Heathcliff's hatred, we also see his love, if we see Isabella and Hindley suffering, we also see Heathcliff suffering, if we see his inhumanity in revenge, we see the same thing in Hindley, and the same feelings, with different outlet, in Isabella. It is not a scene where Isabella and Hindley are whitewashed and Heathcliff blackened. If the violence of all these passions is unusual in intensity and energy, the balance of sympathy reminds us that these are all human beings. It is also a scene which keeps alive our sense of the beginnings of the action.

After Isabella's story is told, we return to the narrative of Nelly, in the two last sections. Here I just want to pick out a few things to notice. First, the way in which her story moves freely backwards and forwards in time. Nelly tells us about Isabella's death, 'some thirteen years after the decease of Catherine', in an economical fashion, when she is mentioning Heathcliff's questions about his child, and then goes back to pick up the threads of the story 'on the day succeeding Isabella's unexpected visit'. This kind of flexibility is one of the advantages of the personal narration. Another advantage, which this method of narration has in fact in common with the story told in the author's voice, is the opportunity for analysis and reflection. I have said that the resemblances and differences between the characters are illuminating, and in this chapter Nelly explicitly comments on the resemblances and differences in the character and situation of Hindley and Edgar: 'They had both been fond husbands, and were both attached to their children; and I could not see how they shouldn't both have taken the same road, for good or evil.' Her comparison, which is worth looking at, both for what it says and for what it leaves out, is expressed in moral terms: 'They chose their own lots, and were righteously doomed to endure them.' This is followed by a tactful and respectful address to Lockwood, 'But you'll not want to hear my moralising, Mr. Lockwood: you'll judge as well as I can, all these things', after which respect changes to dryness in the delightful touch, 'at least, you'll think you will, and that's the same'. This shows the way in which Emily Brontë keeps the tone varied, keeps the characters of storyteller and listener in mind, and also draws our attention to the diversity of human judgement in this chapter where the point of view and the reader's response keep changing.

Nelly also tells us, with little comment, about Edgar's 'indifference' to Hareton—another aspect of Edgar worth noticing. She speaks in affection and judgement of Hindley, for whom she weeps 'as for a blood relation' and whose death is a blow greater than 'the shock of Mrs. Linton's death'. Nelly's characteristic reactions can be studied here with profit. And there are a few other points worth mentioning: the character and language of Kenneth, one of the few 'minor' characters in the novel, the emphasis on Heathcliff's isolation, the mention of Edgar's withdrawal from social responsibility, and the significant little detail of Hareton's innocent reaction to Heathcliff's grim statement of his intentions: Hareton plays with Heathcliff's whiskers and strokes his cheeks. He is not simply the deprived and depraved child we have seen through Isabella's eyes, hanging the litter of puppies. We cannot say that such details 'look forward' as we might in a conventionally planned novel where the child appears as the father to the man in every sense, preparing us, in the case of young Maggie Tulliver or young David Copperfield, for the adult character and problems. We have already seen both the roughness and kindliness of Hareton, just we as have already seen the 'despot' in the second Catherine. All we can say is that Emily Brontë is keeping her characters consistent: we are moving forward in time as far as the unfolding of action is concerned, but we have begun at the other end with the characters, and in this scene we meet the second generation—Linton and Catherine, at least—for the first time.

This kind of analysis can of course be applied to any chapter, and I have chosen this one not because it is more important than many others but because it is one I have said little about elsewhere, and also because it is one which brings out in detail some of the more difficult problems of the novel, such as the character of Heathcliff, and the sway of sympathy and repulsion. This is an example of analysis, but it is not meant to be exhaustive. You could, for instance, look at the dialogue, which I have not mentioned, and follow up some of the brief points I have made about characterisation. One of the important reasons for close analysis is its reduction of reading-speed. Many people read too quickly, and especially when they are reading novels. What many of us do is to speed through the story—and this is particularly true of an exciting story like *Wuthering Heights*—and then do our literary appraisal with the aid of critics, at some distance from the text. Whenever you read a critic, you should, ideally, test all his conclusion against the detail of the text. The habit of close and slow reading not only means that we read novels carefully, but that we are able to be properly sceptical about other people's opinions and judgements.

FURTHER READING

Note. I have given details of publication only in the case of books which might not be easily accessible in libraries.

1
OTHER WORKS BY THE BRONTËS

Emily Brontë: *The Complete Poems of Emily Jane Brontë* (ed. C. W. Hatfield; contains a brief informative note by Fannie Ratchford on 'The Gondal Story').

Charlotte Brontë: *Jane Eyre; Villette.*

Apart from the general interest of reading these sister novels, there is some profit in making a comparison of their use of fantasy (dreams, ghosts, omens) with that in *Wuthering Heights.* Advanced students might also consider the heroes of all three novels, the treatment of love, the importance of landscape, and the question of realism.

2
WRITINGS ABOUT THE BRONTËS

Margaret Lane: *The Brontë Story; a reconsideration of Mrs. Gaskell's Life of Charlotte Bronte* (level-headed and readable biography).

Winifred Gérin: *Emily Brontë,* OUP 1971, paperback 1978.

Fannie Ratchford: *The Brontës' Web of Childhood* (the authoritative study of the Angrian and Gondal 'legends').

C.P.S: *The Structure of Wuthering Heights* (C. P. Sanger, Hogarth Press, 1926).

Mary Visick: *The Genesis of 'Wuthering Heights'* (Hong Kong, 1958).

3
OTHER NOVELS

The Detached or Apparently Detached Storyteller.
Henry James: *Roderick Hudson*
F. Scott Fitzgerald: *The Great Gatsby.*
Ernest Hemingway: *The First Forty-Nine Stories.*

The Multiple Plot.
Charles Dickens: *Oliver Twist; David Copperfield.*
W. M. Thackeray: *Vanity Fair.*
George Eliot: *Middlemarch.*

The Single Plot.
Jane Austen: Any of her novels.
Charlotte Brontë: *Jane Eyre; Villette.*
George Eliot: *Silas Marner.*
Thomas Hardy: *Under the Greenwood Tree.*
(George Eliot and Hardy may also be compared with Emily
Brontë in their use of landscape).

4
WRITINGS ABOUT THE NOVEL

Wayne Booth: *The Rhetoric of Fiction* (For advanced
students and teachers).

E. M. Forster: *Aspects of the Novel* (Of general interest but
students of Emily Brontë should look at the Chapters on Fantasy
and Prophecy).

Barbara Hardy: *Tellers and Listeners: the Narrative
Imagination,* Athlone Press, 1975.

Percy Lubbock: *The Craft of Fiction* (The classical study of
narrative 'point of view', for advanced students and teachers: a
valuable but limited approach which is excellently balanced by
Wayne Booth's study).

Kathleen Tillotson: *The Tale and the Teller* (an inaugural
lecture published by Rupert Hart-Davis, 1959).